Focus and Thrive

Executive Functioning
Strategies for Teens

FOCUS & THRIVE

EXECUTIVE FUNCTIONING STRATEGIES

for Teens

TOOLS TO GET ORGANIZED, PLAN AHEAD, AND ACHIEVE YOUR GOALS

Laurie Chaikind McNulty, LCSW-C

ROCKRIDGE
PRESS

To Tim, whose support made this possible. And to Molly and Lucy, who always know what to say despite the fact that they are dogs.

Interior and Cover Designer: Mando Daniel
Photo Art Director/Art Manager: Tom Hood
Editor: Erum Khan
Production Editor: Ashley Polikoff

Illustrations © 2020 Mando Daniel, cover; YouWorkForThem Design Studio, pp. x, 22, 86.

ISBN: Print 978-1-64739-651-0 | eBook 978-1-64739-652-7

R0

CONTENTS

Letter to Parents

Dear Parents,

I have been lucky enough to serve as an ally to countless teens as they strengthen their executive functioning skills. These bright, enthusiastic kids come to me when they are facing difficulties getting organized, planning ahead, and starting tasks. You, too, likely recognize your child's strengths as well as their challenges, and chose this book as a means of supporting them through these types of struggles.

As a licensed clinical social worker, I began my work in schools and children's hospital outpatient centers before moving into a private practice. I specialize in supporting positive developmental growth in children from birth into young adulthood. My hope with this book is to help teens gain a deeper understanding of their strengths, as well as their areas for growth.

I have seen firsthand how hard it can be to support your child through these challenges, especially when they're discouraged or wonder why they have to work harder than their peers to accomplish similar tasks. This book is as much for you as it is for your teen. Think of it as your guide to teaching simple, accessible strategies. When you come up against a difficulty, use this book as a reference to find tips and tricks to help you and your teen get unstuck.

To help you achieve a better understanding of executive functioning challenges, I've developed a list of questions for you to reflect on. Take a look at them to evaluate your own executive functioning skills, and check off the points that apply to you. Like all assessments in this book, this is not meant to be a diagnostic tool, but rather a way to gain insight into your own strengths and growth areas.

o When I'm very busy or overwhelmed, I have difficulty prioritizing where to start.

o I struggle to keep my organization systems in place. There are times when I don't have a system at all.

o Planning ahead isn't easy for me. I usually don't have a concrete plan, or I complete tasks at the last minute.

o I can be rigid once I set my mind to something. I have trouble thinking flexibly or changing my plans.

o I often forget items on my to-do list, activities, or plans that I've made.

o I often feel scattered and tend to lose things.

o I'm often late to events or appointments.

o It's hard for me to stay calm when I'm annoyed or upset. I find regulating my emotions a challenge.

o I regularly follow my impulses and act without thinking. I can see that I don't always think things through before jumping in.

o Getting started on tasks can be a challenge for me, especially when I don't find them interesting.

o I find it hard to monitor my progress. I tend to be surprised when I am not meeting my goals or when someone is irritated with me.

You may be surprised by how many areas of executive functioning you and your teen have in common—both strengths and challenges. Recognizing your own areas for growth may assist you in relating to your child as they work to develop new skills.

I find myself continuously inspired by families who develop resilience and build their executive functioning skills. I've written this book for them and for you, with the goal of sharing the tools that I've found to be helpful in my practice over the past decade. As your teen works to implement these strategies into their lives, my sincere hope is that they gain confidence, discover their strengths, and experience the ongoing growth of their executive functioning skills.

Warmly,

Laurie Chaikind McNulty, LCSW-C

Letter to Teens

Dear Teens,

I work every day to support people in meeting their goals, including growing and developing executive functioning skills. What are executive skills? Simply put, they're actions like getting organized, making plans, focusing, paying attention, and even starting on tasks. I've worked for a decade with teens and young adults like you who are looking to improve their executive functioning skills and feel more confident in tackling everyday challenges.

I know that it can be frustrating to feel like you have to work twice as hard to do what seems to come naturally to your friends and classmates. That's why it's so important for me to convey that this book is not about flaws or finding things that need be fixed. Instead, it's meant to serve as a reference guide for you to find your strengths and grow your executive functioning skill set.

This book is *not* about changing who you are or giving you complicated techniques. My aim is to provide you with easy, doable tools that will help you feel more in control of how you run the business of your life. Practical solutions should help you feel less stuck and more confident. You'll learn strategies like how to study efficiently for a big exam and how to navigate a group project. I'll also give you realistic tips for getting your stuff organized and keeping it that way. We'll talk about taking breaks, adding rewards into your routine, dealing with feelings, managing your impulses, planning ahead, and more. My hope is that as you practice these techniques, you will experience success and increased confidence in tackling everyday challenges.

As you work to grow your executive functioning skills, keep in mind the strengths you possess, like creativity, inventiveness, laser focus, perseverance, and spontaneity. By adding new executive functioning tools to your inherent strengths, you'll see just how far you can go.

Warmly,
Laurie

How to Use This Book

This book is meant to serve as a resource, kind of like a toolbox you can pull from as needed. You can read the book straight through from front to back, or skip around to the parts that are most relevant to you. When you're experiencing a challenge, open the pages to find specific strategies for that situation. Don't worry about memorizing anything. Instead, I recommend you pick up this book and use it as a guide for the support you need, when you need it.

Keep in mind that there are several downloadable tables, checklists, and calendars with information you may want to integrate into your routine. Feel free to print as much as you want from callistomediabooks.com/focusandthrive. And remember to keep a pencil and paper on hand so you can practice different techniques as you go.

The Deal with Executive Functioning

Before we get started, it's important to create a shared language around the topic of executive functioning. Part 1 of the book explains what we mean by this term and explores important executive skills. We'll cover some common misconceptions, and we'll also bust some myths about executive functioning. You'll learn all about your executive functioning skills and how you use them.

A lot of people call executive functioning "EF" for short. If you hear a parent, teacher, coach, or therapist say "EF" in the context of paying attention, getting organized, or controlling impulses, they're probably talking about executive functioning skills.

What Is Executive Functioning?

Executive functioning, or EF, is simply a set of skills that allows us to operate efficiently. Harvard researchers describe EF as an "air traffic control system" that attempts to smoothly manage the multiple, over-lapping intellectual and emotional tasks we deal with every day. I like to think of EF as the CEO of our brains, who uses advanced skills to successfully run the business of our everyday lives. This includes:

- Gathering relevant information

- Filtering out distractions

- Assessing situations to determine the best course of action

- Remembering important details

- Planning

- Organizing

- Controlling impulses

- Juggling our busy lives without dropping too many balls

- Helping manage and regulate our emotions

These, plus a few more detailed in the next section, make up our executive function skill set. For everyone, this skill set strengthens over time through years of practice. The process begins when we're babies and continues well into young adulthood. Research shows that the part of the brain in charge of EF—the prefrontal cortex, which is located directly behind your forehead—keeps developing all the way until our mid-20s.

It's important to realize that executive functioning skills are *not* related to intelligence. In fact, countless smart, successful adults struggle with EF and have created systems that work well for them. The more you practice EF skills and build strategies that work for you, the stronger they become. Learning and developing these techniques improves your EF and increases your confidence in navigating life's complexities.

Executive Functioning Skills in a Nutshell

To help you fully understand executive functioning, this section will describe the various skills that make up the brain's "air traffic control system." As you read through these definitions, keep in mind that most people have areas of strength as well as room for growth in each skill. Like most things in life, EF is not all-or-nothing.

Organizing, Planning, and Prioritizing: Figuring out the most relevant information, filtering out unimportant stimuli, deciding what to do first, creating a plan to complete tasks, and being able to organize both our physical space and our thoughts.

Flexible Thinking: Shifting from one idea to another (i.e., going with the flow when you need to), and moving from one task to another (i.e., transitions). This can also include seeing things from multiple points of view.

Working Memory: The ability to hold on to and remember information while also manipulating information in our minds. For example, imagine baking and studying at the same time. You would use working memory to remember how long the cake needs to stay in the oven (holding on to an idea) and for how long to extend the timer if it isn't done after that time (manipulating info). While the cake bakes, you'd also study for your test (remembering info even when you're distracted).

Emotion Regulation: Our capacity to tolerate, understand, and manage our feelings in a way that feels healthy and productive.

Self-Monitoring: Reviewing and thinking about our actions to figure out how we're doing. This helps us assess if we're on the right track and redirect or change course if needed.

Impulse Control: The ability to stop ourselves from acting on impulses (i.e., thinking things through before acting).

Task Initiation: Getting started on tasks, particularly ones we don't want to do.

Now that we have a shared language, we'll look at how each of these EF skills fits into your real life.

Getting Organized, Planning Ahead, and Prioritizing

I like to think of getting organized as the precursor to both planning and prioritizing. Getting organized means knowing where your physical things are (like your phone and books) and giving an order to how you think about your day (for example, first there's school, then music or sports practice, and then dinner and homework).

Once you're organized, you'll find it easier to make a plan. Planning requires us to slow down and spend time thinking about how exactly we want to accomplish goals. Goals can be short-term, like completing your math homework by 9:00 p.m., or long-term, like getting into your top choice for college.

The next step to any good plan is prioritizing. This means figuring out the most important information and planning around that—what to do first, what do to next, and knowing when to start it all.

Everyday life presents lots of distractions, and it can feel stressful as you try to follow through with your plans. For example, if you find it boring to write the English essay you planned to start this afternoon, you could easily let distractions interfere and send you off track. It may also be hard to prioritize that essay when you have other pressing assignments and activities, like studying for a history test, running in the track meet, and going to your friend's birthday party.

By practicing the EF skills of organizing, planning, and prioritizing, it'll be easier to pick out what's important, make a plan, and stick to it. It's important to remember that you don't have to do this alone. Asking a friend or adult to be a sounding board can be very helpful when you're busy or overwhelmed and can't figure out where to start.

Throughout part 1, you'll find self-assessments like the one beginning on this page. These are not meant to provide diagnoses or exact data. Rather, self-assessments are meant to give you an idea about the areas in which you thrive and those in which you would benefit from some practice.

Self-Assessment: Organizing, Planning, and Prioritizing

Read each statement and circle "True" or "False."

True | False—I often lose things or forget where I put them.

True | False—I usually leave the house without everything I need for the day.

True | False—When someone asks me what I think is the most important task on my to-do list, I usually don't know what to say.

True | False—I get lost in the details and tend to miss the bigger picture.

True | False—When someone asks me what my plan is, I don't really have one.

True | False—I procrastinate until the last second and get overwhelmed.

True | False—My room/backpack/locker and other spaces tend to be a mess.

True | False—I have an organization system, but I can't seem to keep it up.

BUSTING MYTHS

EF skills are often misunderstood. Let's explore some common myths and clear up a few misconceptions, too.

Myth: People tell me that I could focus if I wanted to. They say, "You claim focusing is hard, but you can focus on the things you like, like video games. Clearly you're just lazy and unmotivated." Maybe they're right.

Truth: *Actually, many teens with executive functioning difficulties do something called "hyperfocus," giving singular, intense attention to rewarding activities. They may also have difficulty shifting attention from one area of focus to another. However, this does not negate the fact that it's actually hard to concentrate on tasks you don't find enjoyable. Just because you're able to spend four hours practicing your favorite sport, this does not mean you're lazy when it comes to homework.*

True | False—I have trouble figuring out what is most important and where to start.

True | False—My planner mostly stays empty, and I forget to check it even if I do write down my assignments.

Take a moment to review your results by going back and thinking about the answers you marked as "true." Notice your areas of strength as well as areas where you can grow and develop in this EF skill.

Myth: I just do better when I decide things spontaneously. Planning ahead wouldn't help anyway, because I can't follow through with anything.

Truth: *We often make the mistake of confusing outcome-based goals with actions. We say, "I'll do my work ahead of time for this paper" (an outcome-based goal) instead of "I'll write twenty minutes for three nights each week before the paper is due" (an action plan to get us to our goals). If we make concrete goals and learn to be flexible when things don't work out, then we can find ways to plan that work for us.*

Myth: My brain is the way it is. I'm just not the kind of person who has good executive functioning skills.

Truth: *Yes, it's true that the brain plays a large role in EF challenges. However, research shows that working on these skills can lead to improvement and better self-regulation.*

Being Flexible

Being mentally flexible is the ability to shift our thoughts, emotions, plans, and actions based on new data. It does not mean always going with what other people want and giving up your opinions. Rather, thinking flexibly allows us to at least consider new ideas, think about different ways of doing things, and be open to other people's opinions without immediately shutting down. It requires us to go with the flow if our plan isn't exactly working out by shifting from one idea to another. This also includes transitions—such as stopping something fun, like video games, to move to something we don't want to do, like homework.

Consider this: It's Friday night and you have long-standing plans to go to the mall with your friends. You're pumped because you've have been looking forward to the new superhero movie for months. But right before the show, your best friend asks you to hang around the food court instead. Do you change your plans and be flexible, or do you insist on seeing the movie as planned?

A good way to decide is to think about what's most important to you, and how big of a deal the shift is. In this scenario, is it more important to see the movie or hang out with your friend? Would it feel completely wrong to wait until the next day to see it, or do you have to get it in tonight, so nobody spoils it at school the next day? The truth is, there's no right answer, and it depends on your priorities. However, being flexible means that you're better equipped to consider different opinions; being flexible helps you conquer the inconveniences life throws at you.

Self-Assessment: Flexible Thinking

Put a check by the statements that apply to you.

o   I'm pretty set in my ways.

o   People often tell me I need to chill out or let things go.

o   I have set expectations in my mind and tend to get upset when they're not met.

o   I'm not good at compromising.

o   I often feel extremely disappointed when things don't go my way.

o   I have a strong negative reaction to people expressing beliefs different from mine.

o   In group projects, my way is usually the right way, even if other people don't think so.

o   Once I have it in my mind to do something, I get fixated.

o   It's hard for me to move from one activity to another, especially when I have to do something I don't like.

o   I don't like change.

This assessment highlights the ways in which flexible thinking impacts daily life. Notice the answers you checked off, as these may be areas for growth. Reviewing this may also help highlight the strengths you have in this skill.

Holding on to Information

Think of the following three categories of memory: long-term, short-term, and working memory. Long-term refers to the stored memories from your past, like your first day of kindergarten. Short-term is more recent information you can keep in mind and call up quickly if you need it, like the drills your coach just asked you to do in practice. Working memory allows you to hold information in your mind and change it given the context of what you're using it for. EF skills rely heavily on this third type, working memory.

Let's say you're making lasagna. Long-term memory helps you recall the first time you had your grandmother's lasagna at a family dinner when you were five. Short-term memory helps you remember all the ingredients when you go to the store. Working memory makes sure that you put the information to use: remembering that you need salt, knowing that you have to add a bit more than the recipe says to get it just right, and tasting the sauce to know if you added it yet. Working memory also helps your brain remember that you shouldn't take too long because you also have to spend time tonight studying for your science test.

We can relate this to how you might think about your schoolwork. Let's say it's Monday, and you remember that your English paper is due on Friday. You may also remember that you have practice three days this week and a track meet on Thursday. Without working memory, it would be hard to make sure you get everything done.

Self-Assessment: Working Memory

Put a check by the statements that apply to you.

- o I often forget what step I'm on when doing large projects.

- o I rarely remember my schedule for the week without writing it down.

- o People get annoyed when they need to repeat things they just said because I forgot.

- o I have a hard time solving problems in my mind because I can't keep everything straight.

- o I make mistakes because I can't remember if I've done something or not.

- o I live in the present moment and tend to forget that I have other stuff to do.

- o When someone asks about my day, I get embarrassed because I honestly don't remember.

- o Most of the time when I'm not following directions it's because I forgot what they were.

Review the checked-off boxes in this self-assessment. They will help you understand how working memory impacts your daily life, and ways in which you already thrive in this area.

Dealing with Strong Emotions

Emotion regulation refers to the ability to tolerate, manage, and deal with feelings in a productive way. When we're "dysregulated," it can feel like emotions get in the way of everyday things, including being with friends, studying, and acting the way we want to.

The thing about our feelings is that even tough ones are there for a reason. Visualizing this can help you understand the purpose and function of emotions—think of your feelings as lights on the dashboard of a car. The emotion lights pop up to let us know something is going on with us internally, just as the dashboard lights indicate that something is going on with your car under the hood. Emotion regulation is the mechanic who assures us that every issue, no matter how unpleasant, can be dealt with.

We regulate ourselves in several ways, including talking to others, taking care of ourselves when we need a break, thinking things through, and accepting our emotions without being too hard on ourselves. This is a lifelong journey, though it's important to know that adolescence is a key time for brain development and growth in this skill. The American Academy of Child and Adolescent Psychiatry reports that as teen brains develop, the part that drives emotions grows faster than the thinking and coping centers. This means that when we're teenagers, feelings tend to be strong, and it takes the regulating center of our brain longer to catch up.

Interestingly, emotion regulation is often significantly easier with the support of others who are calm and trustworthy, like family and friends. Next time you feel overwhelmed, consider talking to someone you trust to help you through.

Self-Assessment: Emotion Regulation
Read each statement and circle "True" or "False."

True | False—I have trouble telling how big of a deal things are.

True | False—I get really mad when things don't go my way.

True | False—I go from a little frustrated to very angry quickly.

True | False—When I'm excited about something I often get carried away and lose track of what I was supposed to be doing.

True | False—When something bad happens, or I get annoyed, I don't feel like I'm in control of my emotions.

True | False—I often feel out of control of my emotions.

True | False—Things don't seem to get to other people the way they get to me.

True | False—I'm often embarrassed and get angry at myself for the way I manage my emotions.

True | False—I get so happy about the good things that they're all I can think about, and I forget everything else I need to do.

Take a moment and think about how the questions you marked as "true" impact your daily life as you work to regulate your emotions. You may use this as a tool to notice your strengths in coping with challenging feelings.

Thinking Things Through and Making Adjustments

Impulse control requires us to stop and think before acting, which is easier said than done. Many times, we realize we should have thought about our decisions only after we've done something we regret. This EF skill provides an internal check system, like an alarm, that buzzes us and says, "Hang on! Is that the best idea?" Some people tell me that they feel something in the pit of their stomach or a tingling in their fingers that sends a red flag to their brains, giving them a few seconds to think before acting.

The ability to recognize and listen to that alarm is called self-monitoring—checking in with ourselves (and others) to make sure we're acting the way we want to. We want to make sure we're moving toward our goals, instead of away from them.

Imagine that you're listening to music as you study for your history test. A catchy song comes on, and you remember that you've been wanting to post a dance video online, so you take a study break. Two hours later you've achieved perfect choreography, but you're no closer to knowing the years of the Ottoman Empire. Self-monitoring allows you to recognize that you've veered off track, and impulse control will help you think about better choices. (Bonus: Working memory will remind you that you have a test to study for, and flexible thinking will help you shift away from your dance back toward your textbook.)

Self-Assessment: Impulse Control and Self-Monitoring

Put a check by the statements that apply to you.

o   I get easily distracted.

o   I have trouble stopping myself from blurting out or interrupting.

o   I tend to act first and think second.

o   I do things without thinking about the consequences.

o   I'm often surprised by the results on my papers and tests.

o   I don't really know where I stand with my grades unless someone tells me to check.

o   I don't follow up on my assignments or grades regularly.

o   People often ask me, "What were you thinking?"

o   It's hard for me to stop myself from doing something fun, even if I know it's a bad idea.

o   It's hard to know how my relationships are going.

This self-assessment is meant to help you think about your impulse control and self-monitoring. Take a look at the items you checked off to determine areas of growth, and make sure to highlight your current capabilities in this area.

Getting Started

"Task initiation" simply means being able to get started. It sounds easy, but anyone who's faced a long-term project or reading assignment knows just how daunting getting started can be.

Studies show that for those with EF challenges, uninteresting tasks are less rewarding. It becomes more difficult to motivate ourselves with long-term rewards when the short-term task is really boring. For example, the desire for good grades (a long-term reward) doesn't always motivate us to study (a short-term task).

Another hurdle in getting started is worry. A lot of teens I work with say they stress so much about repeating past mistakes that they have trouble beginning new tasks. Take Jay, a college freshman who was in danger of not getting into any of the classes he needed because he didn't register on time. "Last semester, I got really overwhelmed trying to figure out what I wanted to take and when it would all fit into my schedule. I just couldn't even start to solve that puzzle," he told me. "I knew that time was ticking away, but I couldn't get myself to do it. Now that registration is coming up again for this semester, I worry the same thing will happen. I don't even want to think about it." I hear stories like this all the time in my work, and if you relate, you may also be struggling with task initiation.

Self-Assessment: Task Initiation

Rate each statement on a scale of 1 to 5.

1. This never happens.

2. This happens, but rarely.

3. This happens some of the time, but not always.

4. This happens most of the time.

5. This happens all the time.

__ I get started well before things are due.

__ I like to wait until the last minute to start my work.

__ I feel anxious even thinking about beginning a project.

__ I know I should work, but I procrastinate because I know how boring it will be.

__ I can't work up the energy to get started.

__ I think about all the times I've messed up before and would rather do anything else than start my work.

__ I just can't get going, even when I'm not nervous.

Determine how you ranked yourself on each answer. For challenges that arise often, you may find it useful to examine these specific difficulties further. Keep in mind as you review that different circumstances affect how hard or easy it is to get started on a task.

HOW TO ASK FOR HELP

Almost everyone struggles or feels confused some-times. Add in executive functioning challenges, and it's no wonder you may feel tough emotions. The most important thing to do if you're stressed, overwhelmed, or feeling down is to ask for help. Talk to your family, a trustworthy friend, or even a coach or teacher about what you're going through. Therapists and counselors are also available to support you through tough times and are trained to be impartial support systems.

Asking for help can be intimidating. If you're thinking about reaching out but can't quite do it, try this: Ask yourself what you would want your best friend to do if they were feeling like you do, and then take that advice. If you prefer to talk or text for more privacy, there are a lot of resources out there. Below are a few to keep at your fingertips, and you'll find more in the resources at the end of the book.

- **YouthLine** (call 877-968-8491, text "teen2teen" to 839863, or visit OregonYouthLine.org)
- **Crisis Text Line** (text "HOME" to 741741 or visit CrisisTextLine.org/text-us)
- **Teen Talk Mobile App** (download it from TeenLineOnline.org/teen-talk-mobile-app)

STAYING FOCUSED

Attention regulation allows people to choose how to direct their focus, even in the face of distractions, boring tasks, or uninteresting topics. Despite what you may have heard, though, staying focused is not just a matter of willpower. Studies have found that those with executive functioning differences find it more difficult to regulate attention, meaning it's harder to focus on some tasks (usually uninteresting ones) and easier to lose yourself in others (hyperfocus). Practicing the other EF skills we explored will help you harness your attention in ways that work for you.

Self-Assessment: Attention and Focus

Rate each statement on a scale of 1 to 5.

1. This never happens.
2. This happens, but rarely.
3. This happens some of the time, but not always.
4. This happens most of the time.
5. This happens all the time.

___ When I'm doing something fun, I can spend long periods of time hyperfocused without noticing what's going on around me.

— When I focus intently, I have no idea how much time has gone by.

— During school, I feel lost because it's so hard to pay attention.

— I cannot follow what my friends are saying because I'm too easily distracted.

— I find myself daydreaming in class, and then suddenly realize I don't know what's going on.

— I dread doing homework because I can't seem to concentrate on the work.

— I get in trouble with my coaches/teachers for not following directions.

— I need people to repeat things because I wasn't listening.

— My friends look at me funny when we're talking because I'm off topic.

— I worry during timed tests because I spend too much time daydreaming or having a blank mind.

Use this as a tool to assess strengths and challenges in attention and focus. It may help you identify how often you're struggling, and in what areas. The aim is also to illuminate situations in which it's difficult to direct your attention and focus.

Start Strengthening Your Skills

I hope it's clear by now that executive functioning skills take time to practice and develop. Similarly, EF is not binary: You are *not* either great at building EF skills or terrible at it. Strengthening your EF is like building a muscle. The more you train, the stronger you'll get.

You can also focus your efforts to enhance specific EF skills. For example, you may take a look at the self-assessments you took earlier in this section and decide that there are specific skills you'd like to practice more than others. Of course, just like building physical muscles, the results won't be instantaneous. But in the long run, the incremental changes you make will have a more meaningful impact than any instant "perfection" you try to achieve. Celebrate each small victory.

And there's more good news! You're already on your way to success. Just by learning about the specific skills outlined in part 1, you already have a better understanding of yourself. You may notice yourself moving on to the next section with more clarity and confidence. If not, that's okay, too. There's a lot more to learn in the coming pages.

Now that you know more about the essentials of EF, part 2 will teach you step-by-step tools and strategies for building each of these skills.

Key Takeaways:

Executive functioning is a set of skills that help us run our lives smoothly, like our brain's own CEO.

EF skills are not set in stone, but rather can be strengthened with practice and persistence.

EF is not related to intelligence. You can be extremely smart and have room to grow in this domain.

If you are struggling, ask for help. If you aren't sure if you should talk to someone, think about what you would tell your best friend to do.

PART 2

Strategies to Help You Succeed

This part of the book will help you learn specific strategies to successfully tackle daily demands. As you continue to practice, you'll feel more confident at home, school, and beyond. Instead of trying these strategies all at once, pick one or two at a time. The more time you give yourself (and the less you worry about executing them perfectly), the more likely you'll integrate these tools into your daily life.

Getting Ready in the Morning

Morning routines typically include gathering your things for the day, making lunch, showering, brushing your teeth, picking an outfit, and eating breakfast . . . all before 7:00 a.m. You're tired, everyone is in a rush, and it can be hard to get it all done. Here are a few tricks to make the morning chaos run a little smoother.

1. **Make a list.** Start by making a list of each thing you need to do every morning. It helps to have a few empty lines on the bottom of your sheet for add-ons so you can easily update it on any given day. Hang a copy on the door of your room, another one in the kitchen, and one more by the front door so you can review it before you leave the house.

2. **Create a routine.** The more you have a rhythm that feels natural, the easier it will be to get out the door without forgetting anything. Here's an example: Start the night before by making your lunch, picking your outfit, and packing your backpack. In the morning, get ready, check your list, make sure you have everything you need, and get out the door.

3. **Set reminders.** If you have an assignment due at school, set a reminder alert on your phone for the night before to put it in your backpack. Set another timer for 20 minutes before you leave in the morning to make sure you have it.

4. **Get some sleep.** Our biological clocks change when we become teenagers, meaning your body wants to stay up later at night and sleep in later in the morning. This, along with early school start times and the need for about nine hours of sleep each night, can make it tough to get proper rest. Pick a time about nine hours before you have to get up as a "bedtime." If you are staying up late now, move your bedtime 15 minutes earlier each night instead of moving it all at once. This will give your body more time to adjust. If

you're having trouble falling asleep, try turning off screens an hour before bed, taking a warm shower, and meditating.

5. **Stay calm.** Waking up late happens. Take a deep breath and check your list to figure out what you absolutely can't live without that day. If you have only a few minutes, grab assignments that are due that day. Remember your lunch so you won't get hungry later.

Life Hack:
Get creative with alarms. Place your alarm away from your bed so that you have to get up to turn it off. You can also set alarms throughout the morning to remind you to move from one task to another if you tend to get distracted.

Key Takeaways:
Don't panic if something doesn't go according to plan. Prioritize the most important assignments and your lunch before you head out the door.

Planning ahead and using visual reminders like checklists and alarms can help your mornings run smoothly.

Sample Morning Checklist

Take a look at the following sample morning checklist. You can download and print blank versions at callistomediabooks.com/focusandthrive.

- o Shower
- o Brush teeth
- o Contacts/glasses
- o Get dressed and ready
- o Shoes and socks
- o Breakfast
- o Make lunch
- o Feed the dog
- o Walk the dog
- o Pack bag
  - o Lunch
  - o Assignments that are due
  - o Gear for after-school activities
  - o Pens
  - o Paper
  - o Laptop
  - o Books
  - o Phone and charger
  - o Wallet
  - o Keys

Notes:

- _____
- _____
- _____
- _____
- _____
- _____
- _____
- _____
- _____
- _____
- _____
- _____
- _____
- _____
- _____
- _____
- _____

Your Morning Checklist

- ○ _____
- ○ _____
- ○ _____
- ○ _____
- ○ _____
- ○ _____
- ○ _____
- ○ _____
- ○ _____
- ○ _____
- ○ _____
- ○ _____
- ○ _____
- ○ _____
- ○ _____

Notes:

o   _____

o   _____

o   _____

o   _____

o   _____

o   _____

o   _____

o   _____

o   _____

o   _____

o   _____

o   _____

o   _____

o   _____

o   _____

o   _____

Getting Organized

Organizing your space in efficient ways makes it easier for you to find what you need, which in turn makes your whole day run smoother. Everyone organizes their stuff differently, so take some time to find the right way for you.

1. **Clear your workspace.** Clear off your desk and see how much space you have. Make a list of the supplies you need and go shopping.

2. **Get supplies.** Supplies can be a major part of the process, and having what you need can make the task feel a lot more motivating. Find colors and designs that you like and go online for inspiration. Helpful supplies include a file box, folders, labels, markers, pens, pencils, staplers, drawer/desk organizer bins, extra boxes for storage, and hanging folders.

3. **Set up your space.** Once you have supplies, give everything a place.

    • Start with designating a place for each of your items. Label folders, alphabetize your file cabinet, tidy your bookshelf, and assign boxes for your school supplies. (Hint: taking things out of the packaging and putting them into bins makes the space a lot more manageable.)

    • Make a physical folder for each class, and then go through your papers to sort them into the right folder. Do this sorting at least once a week to avoid buildup. Throw away what you don't need. (You can also make digital folders for each class on your computer to sort all your files.)

    • Make an "administrative" folder to store permission slips, calendars, extracurricular schedules, and other paperwork that doesn't go into any of your class folders.

If you feel it's secure, this is a good place to store your login/password info.

- If your space is looking good, show it off! You can also ask for feedback from a friend or family member.

4. **Make it a habit.** Schedule organization time into your weekly routine. Tidying up will become a habit, and your system will be easier to maintain.

Life Hack:
The easier and more efficient your system is in the beginning, the more likely you are to keep it up. Take some time to really think about how to set up a space that works for you.

Key Takeaways:
Find an organization system that makes sense to you.

Make it a habit to maintain your system at a set time every week. It's easier to keep it up by spending a few minutes each week rather than waiting until it is overwhelming.

Making the Most of Your To-Do List

Throughout this book, you'll find lots of recommendations for making to-do lists and writing things down to get organized. Writing things down reduces our stress and helps us remember what we need to do. The point is not to make 100 separate lists, but to find list-making strategies that work for you.

1. **Use what works for you.** This could be writing a list on a piece of paper, using an app, or adding notes to a calendar. (Suggestions for apps are listed in the resources section on page 115.) Here are a few ideas to give you a place to start:

   - Make a list on paper of things to do for the day and post it on your bedroom door.

   - In an app, make sections for school, extracurriculars, social time, and chores.

   - Set up calendar reminders for tasks throughout the week.

   - Create a grid with each day of the week and update it every Sunday (example on pages 50–51).

2. **Clearing your list.** Have a way to signify that you've finished a task. Try checkboxes, crossing things off, or writing "done" next to the task. If you don't get to something in your calendar, make sure you move it to another day or time so you don't forget.

3. **Leave room for notes.** Don't be afraid to make notes on your to-do items. This will help you remember key details. For example, if you need to buy homecoming tickets, write a note about how much they cost so you bring the right amount to pay.

4. **Pick three priorities.** Each day, pick the top three things you want to accomplish. That way you won't feel overwhelmed and will know where to start.

5. **Managing multiple to-do lists.** With everything you have to keep track of in school, home, extracurriculars, and social time, you can end up with more lists and calendars than you have time to check. Try to consolidate them into one list or calendar as much as possible. Only add extra lists for special tasks or more challenging areas (morning routine, submitting an application, etc.).

Life Hack:
While some tasks are time sensitive, you can move others to another day. Flexible thinking will help you be kind to yourself and re-prioritize if unexpected emergencies come up or if you simply don't get everything done.

Key Takeaways:
Find ways to make a to-do list that works for you (a calendar, an app, a paper list, etc.). Make sure you try it for a few weeks to see if it sticks.

Pick a few priorities each day to focus on, and be flexible if plans need to change.

Sample To-Do List

Here is an example to-do list, broken down by activity. The bold items are the top priorities for that day.

School

- **Check planner and online classrooms for assignments (every day)**
- **Check grades (Wednesday and Friday)**
- **Math test (Monday)**
- **Chem lab due (Thursday)**
- English essay draft (30 minutes each day)
- Government reading packet (Tuesday, Thursday)

Basketball

- **Wash uniform (Thursday)**
- **Pump air into the ball (Friday)**
- Practice (Monday–Thursday)
- Game (Saturday)
- Drills (every day)

Religious School

- **Homework (Saturday)**
- Read passages (Tuesday, Wednesday, Thursday)
- Bake sale (Friday)

Chores

- **Clean room (Sunday)**
- **Take out trash (Thursday night)**
- Organize folders and desk (Tuesday, Friday)
- Laundry (Friday afternoon)

Friends

- **Call Arjun about movie after basketball game (Thursday)**
- Text Clara about Chem study group (Sunday)
- See if Blake can hang out next weekend

Homecoming

- **Buy tickets (Tuesday)**
- **Pay Arjun for the limo (Tuesday)**
- Order corsage (Thursday)

Notes:

- **Get red corsage to match outfit**
- **Pack cash in bag to pay Arjun**

Your To-Do List

You can use the examples right from the book or create a personalized system. Check out the **Checking Your Progress (page 72)** or **Getting Chores Done (page 62)** sections to find other ways of remembering your everyday tasks. You can download and print blank lists online at callistomediabooks.com/focusandthrive.

○ _____

○ _____

○ _____

○ _____

○ _____

○ _____

○ _____

○ _____

○ _____

○ _____

○ _____

○ _____

○ _____

- ○ _____
- ○ _____
- ○ _____
- ○ _____
- ○ _____
- ○ _____
- ○ _____
- ○ _____
- ○ _____
- ○ _____
- ○ _____
- ○ _____
- ○ _____
- ○ _____
- ○ _____
- ○ _____
- ○ _____

Doing Homework

Doing homework requires the combined use of several executive functioning skills, like working memory, task initiation, planning, organizing, and emotion regulation, to name a few. Here are some tools to make it a bit easier.

1. **Prioritize assignments.**

   - Start with anything that's due the next day.

   - If there's time left over, think about what you need to do for the rest of the week. For example, if your English paper is due tomorrow, make sure you finish that before starting on the math set that's due in three days.

   - If nothing is due tomorrow and you have some time, get started on the assignment that's due next. You don't know what a teacher may throw at you last minute, and it helps to be ahead.

2. **Find a designated workspace.** It's important to have a clutter-free workspace and minimize distractions. Some people like to do their work alone in their rooms, while others do better in a common family space. You may find that you're most productive outside of the house, at a library or with a study partner.

3. **Set timers and take breaks.** Set one timer for work and a second timer for breaks. An easy plan is 15 minutes on, then 5 minutes off. Plan exactly what you'll do on your break and try to pick activities that are not too distracting so you can get back to work when it's time.

4. **Reward yourself.** Incentives include time with friends, exercising, video games, etc. Match the size of the reward to the size of the task. For smaller tasks, give yourself a

smaller incentive, and for larger tasks, amp it up so you're more motivated.

5. **Ask for help if you need it.** Some people like to get help from their family or teachers, and others prefer to FaceTime with friends. Many find working with tutors to be beneficial. Find out what works for you, and tap into help when you need it.

Life Hack:
One study showed that a 20-minute walk outside helps students pay better attention afterward. Get outside as a break to renew focus.

Key Takeaways:
Our EF is working hard during homework time. Prioritizing, planning, organizing, working memory, impulse control, task initiation, and often emotion regulation are all in play.

Don't try to do all your work at once. Figure out what to prioritize and remember to take planned breaks.

If you're really stuck, think of a reward for finishing your work.

What Do You Think?
Have you ever told yourself you would take a small break and then had trouble getting back to work? Do you think the break activity was too distracting? What activity could you try instead?

Participating in Class Discussions

Volunteering in class requires a lot of executive functioning skills, including working memory to remember what the last person said, flexible thinking to shift as the discussion changes, focus to attend to the topic at hand, and planning so you feel prepared—just to name a few. Emotion regulation is also at play, as speaking in front of the class requires us to feel calm enough to jump in.

1. **Take deep breaths.** First, calm your body. Often, speaking in front of others produces a lot of stress. In these moments, it's helpful to take a few deep breaths to calm your nervous system and reduce the physical feelings of worry. Try 4-4-4 breathing: Breathe in through your nose for four seconds and watch your stomach expand like a balloon. Then hold your breath for four seconds. Finally, breathe out through your mouth for four seconds.

2. **Write down the topic.** In order to help with ongoing attention throughout the discussion, write down key points to focus on. If you keep taking notes, it will be easier to pay attention, and you'll have something to reference if you do zone out for a minute.

3. **Write down what you want to say.** Once you know the topic of the discussion, write down a few points that you want to make in order to feel prepared and reduce stress. Cross out a point if someone else says it and write down new thoughts as they come up. This will help you focus on the conversation and rework your ideas as needed.

4. **Home in on your point.** When people are nervous or excited about a topic, they tend to get carried away, bogged down by the details, or go off on tangents. When speaking, focus on one or two points that you want to get across (writing this down makes it easier to stay on topic). Reading the

body language of your classmates might tell you if you've gone off track. If people begin to lose focus or seem irritated, see if you can wrap up your point by creating one or two summarizing statements.

Life Hack:
Listen to what others are saying and jot down your counterpoints. That way you won't be so worried about what to say next, and you'll be aware if someone else makes your point.

Key Takeaways:
Calm your anxiety by taking deep breaths in through your nose and out through your mouth.

Write things down as a way to focus on what others are saying, as well as what you would like to add to the conversation.

Make sure to keep your thoughts succinct and relevant, and avoid overly focusing on details or going on tangents.

Working on Group Projects

Everyone will have a group project at some point in school. Staying on target as a group often requires a lot of planning and organizing. Think about the tips below to successfully navigate working with other students.

1. **Figure out what you are responsible for.** Before you get started, have a conversation with the group to assign tasks to each member. The project will run more smoothly if each person knows their role throughout the assignment.

2. **Create a clear way to communicate about the project.** Whether in an email chain, a group text, or an in-person meeting, make sure that you and your group have a clear way to communicate about the project. By picking a platform for talking to each other, you may be able to avoid mix-ups and confusion. Putting group discussions in writing (like in an email chain) gives the added bonus of being able to go back and reference what was said. This can be a big help in remembering who's responsible for what and when things are due.

3. **Set times to meet.** As you start the project, set a few times to meet as a group and review progress, if you can. These meetings should be evenly spaced out throughout the duration of the assignment to get everyone on the same page. For example, if you have a group project due in two months, consider having a meeting every two to three weeks. Clarify the purpose of each meeting beforehand so everyone is prepared.

4. **Make a timeline for yourself (and others).** Most students are busy and have multiple assignments going at once. With everyone's varying schedules, it can be hard to recall exactly when pieces of the project are due. Use

a shared calendar app or send meeting invites to ensure that everyone is on the same page regarding the project's timeline. Include all the to-dos for the project, like in-person meetings, conference calls, draft due dates, and final presentations. It will also help keep you on schedule and reduce last-minute rushing.

5. **Set your expectations.** Group projects usually require compromise. However, it can be hard to collaborate when we feel ignored or concerned about progress. Discuss your feelings with friends and family members if you get overwhelmed by group dynamics. Then, focus on the parts of the project you *can* control while trying to let go of the parts you can't. If this becomes very challenging, or you're worried that your grade will suffer, make a private appointment with your teacher to get input.

Life Hack:
Get your materials organized by creating a folder devoted to the project. This can be a physical folder or one on your computer. If there is an email chain, make a folder in your inbox to keep all communications about the project in one place.

Key Takeaways:
Communication is key. Find a system to communicate with your group early and often.

Stay organized with meetings, timelines, and folders.

Focus on what you can control and ask others for help if you begin to feel upset or worried.

Studying for a Quiz or Test

For this strategy, I'm referring to the impromptu kind of test that teachers and professors give with short notice (a day or two), and pop quizzes with no notice at all. Imagine you arrive for class and the teacher tells you that you have a quiz tomorrow, or even right now.

1. **Use calming tools.** Quizzes get everyone's heart racing, but it will be much easier to focus and succeed if you can calm your body and mind. Try the 4-4-4 breathing technique described in the "Participating in Class Discussions" section (see page 40). You can also use self-talk that focuses on positive, calming thoughts. A few that may be helpful in the face of a quiz are: "I know the material, so there is no reason to panic"; "It's okay if this doesn't go that well because this is a small part of my grade"; and, "It's going to be fine, and I just need to take a few deep breaths and do the best I can."

2. **Focus on what you know.** If the quiz has several questions, focus on those you do know the answers to and try your best on the rest. It's better to get full points for the answers you know are right than spend all your time staring blankly at the ones you don't.

3. **Ask for advice.** If you do have some time to prepare, ask the teacher for guidance about what to focus on, and check in with your classmates about what they plan to study. This way, you can spend your time productively by reviewing relevant material.

4. **Let go of perfection.** Most people want to do as well as they can on quizzes and tests. It can be stressful to have a surprise quiz without time to prepare, and even more stressful to feel as though you need to study everything in just one night. Know that in situations like this, all you can do is try. Plus, working to memorize everything you've learned

throughout the semester can get in the way of focusing on the materials you actually do need to review.

Life Hack:
Make sure to ask the teacher about the format of the quiz (essay, multiple choice, etc.). That way you know what to expect, which increases your ability to study successfully and decreases stress and worry.

Key Takeaways:
Don't worry about perfection. Try your best and focus on the questions you know.

Talk to your teacher and classmates about where they recommend you focus your study energy.

Take a few deep breaths and use helpful thoughts if worry takes over.

AIDAN'S DAY

Aidan was exhausted Friday morning before school. He stayed up late to finish an assignment at the last minute, and he slept through his alarm. He ran out the door and just caught the bus—a good sign. In his first two classes, he managed to pay attention and understand what was going on. His girlfriend, Liz, even asked him to hang out that weekend with their friends, a great sign since they'd been fighting a little recently. So, by the time he got to English class for third period, he felt like things were turning around.

His English teacher, Ms. Lamar, greeted the class and asked everyone to hand in their papers (the paper Aidan stayed up until one in the morning writing because he'd procrastinated). Aidan suddenly realized it was at home still sitting in the printer, and both his parents were at work. His dad's words echoed in his head: "Aidan, in the real world no one is going to be there to rescue you all the time like Mom and I do." On top of losing points for his paper being late, Aidan remembered that his dad told him he wouldn't be able to go out that weekend if there were any zeros in the online grade portal for his school on Friday afternoon. Liz was going to be angry, and Dad was, too. Aidan was annoyed at himself for forgetting his stuff, angry at the teacher for giving such a dumb assignment, and mad at his dad for being a helicopter parent.

Aidan slipped out of class and walked the halls for 10 minutes. He came back to class when the security guard caught him sitting in the stairwell. The problem now was that he missed the beginning of class and was lost and distracted anyway. *Forget it*, he thought. *I'll just zone out and not listen; not that it matters anyway. I have no social life and I'm failing school.* Liz noticed that Aidan was sort of out of it and asked if she could help. He told Liz about his terrible day, and she ended up giving him some really good advice. She said, "Aidan, you are so smart—you just forgot one assignment. I know your dad is going to be mad, but you can tell him you'll turn it in Monday. I won't blame you if he still won't let you go out. But maybe next time, set an alert on your phone for the morning or write a big sign for your door to REMEMBER the PAPER! I'll text you, too, to help." Aidan thought about it, relieved she wasn't angry and happy to have her support. A few reminders weren't such a bad idea either.

Studying for an Exam

We typically have a longer time to prepare for exams than for quizzes. We know what topics the exams will cover and when they're coming. Most teachers also tell students about the format of the test in advance. Use this information to get a head start, reduce anxiety, and feel prepared on the day of the exam.

1. **Make a schedule.** As soon as you know when the exam will be, add a study schedule to your calendar. Add a few nights at the end of each unit to review your materials throughout the semester. Then, three to four weeks before the exam, study for a few hours at least two days per week. Ramp it up the week of the test, spending time each night reviewing the material. See the graphic organizer on page 54 for an example study schedule to integrate into your calendar.

2. **Use or make a study guide.** If you're given a study guide for the exam, use it, as it will likely contain all the materials you need. To review everything in the guide without getting overwhelmed, break it up and add small chunks to your calendar. If there's no study guide, try making your own. To do this, start with an outline with each topic or unit as a header. Fill it in with key facts, notes from class, and summaries of key readings in bullet point form. You can also add practice questions from old homework or unit quizzes. If this feels overwhelming or you don't know where to start, ask your teacher for guidance about what headers might be most relevant to review.

3. **Know your learning style.** Knowing your learning style can be helpful during exam prep. If you process information by discussion and listening, talk to a friend about the material or even put yourself in a room and talk to yourself. If visual learning helps you, make sure you're writing down the material you're trying to learn. Some people work best

with the kinesthetic style (using touching and movement), so notecards and drawings help. The most important part is not how you do it, but what works best for you. To figure this out, take a learning style quiz online.

4. **Get a good night's rest.** The nights leading up to your exam are crucial. The brain needs sleep and rest to properly function, and working memory is affected by sleep patterns. In your schedule, plan to stop working at least one hour before you want to fall asleep, to give yourself time to wind down and get ready for bed. If worry about the exam keeps you up, try guided meditation.

Life Hack:
Spread out your studying. Cramming is a fact of life, but if you can pace yourself over the period of a few weeks, you will reduce your stress and increase the efficiency of your study sessions.

Key Takeaways:
Do not try to study all at once. Rather, plan out a study schedule to feel less overwhelmed and take in information more effectively.

Use your study guides or make one for yourself.

Sample Study Planner

Take a look at the following example planner you can use to get ready for your exams. Fill out the organizer by date, time, and what material you'll study that day. Then, when you're done, check the box to help you remember what you've completed. If you prefer, plan your study times in the calendar you already use. Here's an example of a study planner for a US History exam on the Civil War era. You can download and print blank versions online at callistomediabooks.com/focusandthrive.

Exam: US History — Civil War Era

DATE	TIME	MATERIAL	COMPLETE
Sunday, February 28	2:00–4:00 p.m.	Make study guide outline	√
Monday, March 1	5:00–6:30 p.m.	Civil War generals	√
Wednesday March 3	4:00–6:00 p.m.	Response from President Lincoln/ Gettysburg Address	√
Thursday, March 4	3:00–4:00 p.m.	The Battle of Gettysburg	√
Saturday, March 6	2:00–5:00 p.m.	Battlegrounds/Key battles	
Sunday, March 7	2:00–5:00 p.m.	Key battles—Fort Sumter, Palmito Ranch, Antietam	
Monday, March 8	7:00–8:00 p.m.	Timeline of the war	
Wednesday, March 10	5:00–7:00 p.m.	Review/Email teacher questions	
Friday, March 12	5:00–6:00 p.m.	Review	
Sunday, March 14	2:00–6:00 p.m.	Review	
TEST! Monday, March 15	11 a.m.–History Class	TEST!!	

Your Study Planner

Exam:

DATE	TIME	MATERIAL	COMPLETE

Writing a Paper

When you're writing a paper, it can be helpful to follow a few strategies to make sure you stay on track and get everything done effectively.

1. **Pick a topic.** Figuring out what to write about can be one of the hardest parts of writing a paper. To help the ideas flow, start by taking a blank document and writing down all your ideas in a stream of consciousness manner. (That is, don't worry about what comes out and just write whatever comes to mind about the subject or prompt.) Doing this helps us get unstuck and allows us to let go of the worry that we won't find the "perfect" topic. After you do this, walk away for a little while and decide on a topic a bit later. You can also have a friend or family member look over your ideas to help you pick.

2. **Give yourself time.** Just like in many strategies outlined in this book, a timeline is helpful to make sure you finish on time and reduce the stress of last-minute rushing.

3. **Use an organizer.** Use an organizer to outline your paper. This will create a clearer vision of the main points, ease the flow of your paper, and help you stay on track and work efficiently. See page 54 for a brief example.

4. **Reward yourself and take breaks.** Writing requires sustained focus and the creation of novel material. In order to maintain your stamina, make sure you are giving yourself small rewards throughout the process. Many students will work for 15 to 30 minutes at a time and then go on their phones for 5 to 10 minutes. Be mindful that breaks should not be so distracting that it is impossible to get back to work. Set alerts on your phone to remind you when your time is up.

Life Hack:

Writing can feel very difficult when we're trying to get things just right. To help your writing flow, put all your ideas on paper without stopping to evaluate your words, and then edit later. This will help you overcome writer's block.

Key Takeaways:

Don't worry about being perfect the first time around. Get something down on paper and edit later to ease the flow of writing.

Use a graphic organizer to help with the structure of your paper.

Set a timer with breaks to maintain your focus over the long term.

Sample Writing Graphic Organizer

This is an example of a graphic organizer for writing an opinion paper. The type of organizer you use largely depends on the type of paper you're writing. Ask your teacher or look online for the style of organizer that fits your specific paper. You can download and print blank versions online at callistomediabooks.com/focusandthrive.

Introduction: Give a few sentences with background and introduce your opinion. Outline what you're going to say

Reason 1: Give evidence to back up your claim.

Reason 2: Give evidence to back up your claim.

Reason 3: Give evidence to back up your claim.

Conclusion: Reiterate your opinion. Write a few sentences summarizing your argument with a concluding sentence.

Your Writing Graphic Organizer

What do you want to write about?

o _____

Introduction:

Reason 1:	Reason 2:	Reason 3:

Conclusion:

Submitting an Application

Applications precede admission to meaningful experiences in our lives, like college, internships, or competitions. We therefore place a lot of importance on these applications, making them both exciting and stressful. Follow a few tips to help the process feel more manageable.

1. **Gather required documents.** Applications usually require several items other than demographic info and essays, such as transcripts, copies of diplomas, and letters of recommendation. Many of the supplemental materials take time and energy to obtain, so start by getting them as soon as possible.

2. **Figure out a timeline.** Get a timeline on your calendar and set three alerts for each item (two days before, a day before, and the day of) to remind yourself of upcoming tasks and submission deadlines.

   - **Two months prior to due date.** Begin your work at least eight weeks before the deadline. At this time, gather supplemental documents, read through the entire application so you get a sense of the whole process, and fill out the demographic information (name, address, date of birth, etc.).

   - **Six weeks prior to due date.** Consider essay topics (if applicable) and make short outlines.

   - **Three to five weeks prior to due date.** Draft your essays and check in on the status of your supplemental documents to make sure they're on their way. Three weeks before the deadline, edit your writing and ask a friend or family member to take a look at your work for feedback.

- **One to two weeks prior to due date.** Make final changes to essays and put all of your supplemental documents in one place. If applications are online, begin uploading what you need to the website.

- **Three days before deadline.** Make sure everything is in a folder to mail or be uploaded to the right place. Gather any remaining materials. This will give you a day or two of wiggle room in case there are last minute changes or urgent matters.

- **The day before the deadline.** Ask a family member or friend to double-check that you have everything you need. An extra pair of eyes is always helpful, especially when we're stressed. Go to the post office if needed and mail the application with a tracking number. If online, submit electronically.

3. **Get help when you need it.** It's helpful to ask for feedback and support as you work on an application. Try asking a friend who's familiar with the school or program you're applying to, or check in with a family member or teacher who can review your essays and materials to make sure everything is accurate.

Life Hack:
Send a follow-up email to the people making the admissions decisions after you turn in the application, especially if you've met them in person. This may simply read "I have submitted my application and look forward to hearing from you. Thank you for this opportunity."

Key Takeaways:
Don't wait until the last minute, particularly for documents you need to request, such as transcripts and references.

Make a timeline in advance to reduce stress, rushing, and mistakes.

Making an Appointment

As you get older, it may become your responsibility to schedule visits to your doctor, dentist, hairstylist, guidance counselor, or tutor, to name a few. Use the following guidelines to help you make appointments.

1. **Do some research.** Look up the place of business and check when they are open, get the phone number, and figure out the physical location. Talk to your parent beforehand about good times to go so that you have multiple options of dates and times for your appointment.

2. **Pick a time.** Plan a time of day to call when the place of business is open.

3. **Practice what you'll say.** Practice the conversation with your parent if you're nervous, and make sure they're around in case you need help or questions come up.

4. **Place the call.** Tell the receptionist why you're calling. For example, you could say, "I need to make an appointment for my yearly physical with Dr. Smith," or, "My tooth has been hurting and I need to see the dentist."

5. **Confirm the details.** Before you hang up, confirm the date and time of your appointment, the address, what you need to bring, and what time you'll need to get there. If your appointment is virtual, make sure you have the link to the video chat or the phone number to call.

6. **Get there early.** Plan to arrive 10 minutes early in case you need to park or fill out paperwork. For virtual visits, sign on to your computer or phone a few minutes beforehand to make sure everything is working.

7. **Bring your wallet.** You might need to pay afterward.

8. **Follow up.** If needed, make a follow-up appointment before you leave and put it in your calendar with a reminder alert.

Life Hack:
Enter your appointment time in your calendar in your phone. Set reminders for two days before, a day before, an hour before, and the time you need to leave to avoid forgetting.

Key Takeaways:
Make sure you know why you're requesting the appointment, what time you would like it to be, and what you need to bring.

It's normal to be nervous when making appointments, especially in the beginning. Have a parent close by if needed, and don't be embarrassed to practice beforehand.

Make sure to write down your appointments and set reminders to leave on time.

What Do You Think?
Does making appointments for yourself feel like no big deal, or is it intimidating? What do you think might make it easier? A script? Practice? Making appointments online when you can?

Cleaning Your Room

Having a clean room makes it easier to find items quickly and without a headache. Still, tidying can feel like a hassle, especially when it's boring. Try a few of these tools to help simplify and speed up the process.

1. **Break your room down into areas and clean them one at a time.** An easy way to do this is to pick a piece of furniture and start there.

   - Bed: Try to make your bed once a day. If you don't have time in the morning, do it when you get home from school. It's a small accomplishment to feel good about, and it creates a surprising sense of calm when you are in your room.

   - Under your bed: If you have space under your bed, get long containers to store items you don't use often.

   - Desk: Check out the "Getting Organized" section for tips on tidying your desk (see page 30).

   - Closet: Separate your closet by type of clothing (sweaters, pants, shirts, etc.). If you haven't worn something in six months and don't need it for special occasions, consider donating or selling it. Put away your laundry within 24 hours of it coming out of the dryer.

   - Floor: Keep your floor as clear as possible. This will instantly make the room feel tidier. Get an extra hamper or more storage containers if needed.

   - Bookshelf: Stand books up rather than stacking them on the shelf. Declutter your books by donating the ones you don't need to the local library.

- Dresser: Know what goes in each drawer (one for shirts, one for socks, etc.). Try folding your clothes within a day of them coming out of the dryer to avoid pileup and reduce wrinkles. Even if you don't fold clothes, put them in the right drawer so you can find your things easily and quickly.

- Miscellaneous items: Get boxes. Boxes allow you to put things away and have your room feel tidy without having to spend a lot of time organizing. Go through each box and tidy up once a week.

2. **Do small "power cleans" a few times a week.** Pick at least three days (e.g., Sunday, Tuesday, and Thursday) to do a power clean. Set a timer for 5 to 10 minutes on each of those days, and tidy as much as you can in that time. If it helps, pick a reward or fun activity for when you're done.

Life Hack:
Start a junk drawer. Use it for miscellaneous items and other knick-knacks that don't have a place, and simply close the drawer. Your room will feel decluttered and the effort is minimal.

Key Takeaways:
Don't wait to clean. Instead, try short and fast power cleans a few times each week.

Clean one area of your room at a time to avoid feeling overwhelmed.

Getting Chores Done

Most teens have at least a few required chores besides cleaning their rooms, like taking out the trash and recycling, washing dishes, or doing their laundry. No matter the task, it can be helpful to have a plan to get yourself going and avoid feeling overwhelmed.

1. **Include chores in your weekly routine.** Try to do the same chore on the same day, if possible, to avoid stressing and using extra brainpower. See if you can pick days that feel logical to you. For example, if the trash is picked up every Friday morning, round up the trash every Thursday evening. If you're supposed to clean your room once a week, and you tend to have more free time on Sundays, then set aside an hour each week on Sunday to tidy up.

2. **Multitask.** To maximize time, get a few things going at once. Try washing the dishes while your food is heating up in the microwave, making your bed while your clothes are drying, or calling a friend while you're walking the dog. That way you can use your time efficiently and not feel like you're spending all day on housework. If you find this too distracting, you can always cut back to one thing at a time.

3. **Set a timer for a blitz round of chores.** Pick a certain amount of time you'd like to spend on your chores, set a timer, and race yourself to see how much you can get done before the buzzer sounds. You might be surprised by how quickly you can do chores when working against a clock. This also motivates you to get started since you know there's a definite end time.

4. **Make it automatic.** The more you practice something, the more automatic it becomes and the less brainpower it requires. For example, the first time you do laundry, you have to think about how to separate the clothes, how much detergent to use, what cycle to set, and when to come back to move the clothes to the dryer. However, the more you do it, the more your autopilot will take over. Eventually, you may even run through the steps without thinking about it. Bonus: The less taxing it is, the easier it may be to get started.

Life Hack:
Set a recurring alert on your phone with the time and day of the week you'd like to do each chore. After you're done with chores, reward yourself with something fun.

Key Takeaways:
Break chores down by making them into routines and picking days for each chore.

Get chores done faster by combining them or by doing something fun while you're working.

What Do You Think?
Have you ever told yourself you'd do a chore and then not gotten around to it? What types of reminders and rewards might help you follow your plan and complete your work?

Sample Chore Table

Take a look at the following example planner to incorporate chores into your daily schedule. You can use this on its own as a checklist to hang in your room or on your fridge, or you can add items into the calendar you already use. Below is a completed example. You can download and print blank versions online at callistomediabooks.com/focusandthrive.

DAY	CHORES
Monday	• Collect and take out recycling • Dishes after dinner
Tuesday	• Bring in recycling bins • Dishes after dinner
Wednesday	• Dishes after dinner
Thursday	• Collect and take out trash • Dishes after dinner
Friday	• Cook dinner • Run the dishwasher
Saturday	• Laundry—wash and fold
Sunday	• Dishes after dinner • Clean room

Your Chore Table

DAY	CHORES
	• • • • •
	• • • • •
	• • • • •
	• • • • •
	• • • • •
	• • • • •
	• • • • •

LEILA'S DAY

Leila, a tenth grader, came to see me after getting into a massive fight with her parents for saying she would do chores around the house but never following through. "I know I need to actually do stuff, but it's really boring and I'm not interested. Plus, half the time I forget like five minutes after they ask me. Don't get me wrong. It's not that I want to fight with them, and I hate the yelling, but it almost feels like I can't physically get myself to get started."

This is not an unusual problem in my practice. Getting chores done combines several executive functions, such as task initiation, working memory, flexible thinking, prioritizing, self-monitoring, and impulse control. That's a lot to ask! I worked for a bit with Leila to strengthen those skills, and we got to the point where she could use some EF tricks to do her chores as quickly and as painlessly as possible.

Leila learned that she needed to write down what her parents asked her to do in her calendar as they were talking so she had an action plan. Otherwise, her parents had to put a list on her door of what needed to get done every afternoon. Leila realized alerts reminding her to get started were helpful, so she used timers to do chores in 10-minute intervals. She said, "it's better to focus for 10 minutes than to think about doing it for an hour and do nothing." Then she could take a break and do something she wanted, which most of the time was texting a friend or going on Reddit for a few minutes.

Leila also thought more flexibly after a bit of success, with her language shifting from "I literally can't do it" to "I really don't like it, but I guess I can when I make it short and know something fun is coming after." She was able to control the impulse to watch YouTube instead of clean and to prioritize chores when she needed to. Leila's parents acknowledged all her hard work, and actually gave her a lot more freedom because they started to trust her more.

Making Plans with Friends

Picture this: It's Friday night and you really want to go to the mall with your friends, but no one is free. Your parents warned you this might happen if you waited until the last minute, but the idea of texting someone was overwhelming. Plus, you totally forgot until it was too late. The following are some tips to help you make plans with friends so that you can hang out when you'd like to.

1.   **Calm your nerves.** If asking friends to hang out makes you nervous, take a deep breath. Worry usually comes from the fear of saying the wrong thing, getting rejected, or not hearing back at all. Try using a helpful, encouraging thought, such as, "This person usually says yes when I ask them to hang out," or, "Even if they're busy, I can always try someone else, or ask again another time. I won't know unless I ask."

2.   **Start with closer friends.** Reach out to people who have responded positively to you in the past. Once you build confidence, you will be better equipped to take bigger risks by texting or calling those you don't know as well.

3.   **Look at your calendar first.** Make sure that you have time to hang out before making plans. Check your calendar and set reminders so you don't let anyone down or have to cancel at the last minute.

4.   **Plan ahead.** If you wait until the last minute, your friends may already be busy. Set a reminder in your phone to reach out two days ahead of time. Try a quick text or direct message that says, "Hey, what are you doing this weekend?"

5.   **Think flexibly.** Before you ask your friends to hang out, think about what everybody likes to do. Considering the interests of others makes them more likely to say yes and will make the experience more fun. Especially in the beginning of a friendship, it can help to be flexible about what

to do or where to go as a way to show your friends that you value them.

6. **Run it by your parent.** It feels awful when you make plans and have to back out because your parent says no. When someone asks you to hang out, use impulse control to say, "Let me ask my parents," before jumping to an immediate yes.

Life Hack:
Text your friends back right away, when possible. That way you won't forget to do it later.

Key Takeaways:
Don't wait until the last minute to make plans, and text back right away to avoid forgetting.

Make sure you're available and that your parents agree before making plans.

Be flexible about what you'll do and when to do it, to increase the likelihood of getting together.

What Do You Think?
What's the hardest part about making plans with friends? Is it getting up the courage to text, figuring out what to say, or something else? How can you plan ahead to feel prepared?

Talking and Listening to Others

It can be tricky to engage in conversation at times, especially when we're practicing our EF skills. Do you ever find yourself easily distracted when talking to a friend—not listening, just waiting for your turn to talk, or even interrupting? Here are a few pointers for making sure that chatting with others goes smoothly.

1. **Notice body language.** Before and during a conversation, monitor the body language of the other person. First, look at their eyes and face: Are they smiling and nodding (showing interest), rolling their eyes or grimacing (becoming annoyed or angry), or looking away (getting bored)? Then look at the rest of their body. Are they backing away, crossing their arms, or tapping their feet? These may be signs that they're not interested. However, if they're leaning in, using hand gestures, and facing you, they're probably as engaged as you are. If you notice body language that's telling you the other person is feeling irritated or not paying attention, you can change the subject, ask a question, or end the discussion politely by saying, "I don't want to keep you. I'll catch up with you later."

2. **Don't get lost in the details.** When you're having a conversation with others, it's easy to get lost in the details, especially if you're discussing a topic you know a lot about. Make sure to leave room for the other person to interject and give their opinions as well.

3. **Show interest and ask questions.** Many times when someone is talking, we're simply waiting for our turn to talk. This works if you're trying to make a specific point, like in a debate, but it may mean the conversation is one-sided and not fun for the other person. Have you ever told a story about your life, only to have your friend immediately launch into their own story without even acknowledging what you

said? Or what about when you're upset and someone says, "That isn't that bad. Let me tell you about something that happened to me!" Even if they think they're helping, it may hurt because it can make us feel like we're not being listened to. To counteract this, ask questions or acknowledge their points. You could say, "That's awesome" or "I have totally been there." Then you can share a relevant anecdote.

Life Hack:
Sometimes we worry that we'll forget what we want to share, which makes it hard to listen and respond. Try saying something like "I want to talk about that, but I'm afraid I'm going to forget something I really want to tell you. Will you remind me of _____?" This lets the other person know that what they're saying is important and allows you to remember your story, too.

Key Takeaways:
Notice body language and change up your conversation as needed.

Make sure you're listening to the other person and responding, rather than just waiting for your turn to talk.

Checking Your Progress (Self-Monitoring)

All of us can easily get caught up in the here and now, follow our impulses, and forget to take a moment to stop and think about how we're doing. However, it's important to check your progress and change course as needed. Examples include looking at your grades weekly to make sure you have all your assignments in, reviewing your work when you're done to find avoidable errors, and talking to a friend who seems to be angry with you. All three of these endeavors involve assessing how things are going and making adjustments if necessary.

1. **Check as you go.** Check your work as you go, especially when it comes to homework, classwork, and tests. To do this, take a few deep breaths after completing your assignment, and then go back to check each problem again to avoid errors due to rushing. If you find yourself rushing through your review, take a break for a minute and then come back to it.

2. **Adding to your calendar/to-do list.** Make sure that you write down reminders to monitor your progress. These can include looking up current grades, checking your bank account, or emailing your math teacher about last week's test. Pick a day each week (I'd suggest Sunday or Monday night) to make sure that everything you have to check is noted on your weekly calendar or to-do list. (Check out the calendar reminders example on pages 74–75.)

3. **Ask someone you trust.** Sometimes we need to monitor ourselves in areas that can't be put on a checklist, like how we're doing in our friendships, or what's going on with someone we like. For questions like those, it can be helpful to talk to someone you trust. Find a friend, sibling, parent,

or counselor to get feedback from to make sure you're on track. Some teens find it helpful to start the conversation by saying, "I think my friend is upset with me—can I ask you about it?" or, "I like her, but I can't read her signals and I don't know if I'm doing it right," or even, "What should I say to him next?" Just because we call it *self*-monitoring doesn't mean you have to do it alone. Outside perspective might be just what you need to figure out where you stand and plan your next move.

Life Hack:

Sometimes when we check in with ourselves and see areas for improvement, we get really hard on ourselves. Try to talk to yourself like you would talk to a friend. Instead of saying "I can't believe I missed that, I'm so annoyed with myself," try flipping it to "I wish I didn't miss that, but good thing I caught it now rather than later."

Key Takeaways:

Check your work as you go, or add self-monitoring items to your calendar/to-do list to make sure you are on the right track.

Don't go it alone. Self-monitoring in relationships is much easier with a few sounding boards.

Sample Self-Monitoring Reminders

Here are some ideas for calendar reminders that you might add to track your progress. You can download and print blank versions online at callistomediabooks.com/focusandthrive.

Sunday

o   Add check-ins to my to-do list. (Math grades, online assignments/grades, English teacher conference, check bank account, track team placement, call Nikki)

Monday

o   Check planner and online classrooms for assignments

Tuesday

o   Check planner and online classrooms for assignments

o   Talk to English teacher to see what I can do about my essay grade last week

Wednesday

o   Check planner and online classrooms for assignments

o   Ask Mom/Dad how much is in my bank account before homecoming

Thursday

- o   Check planner and online classrooms for assignments
- o   Ask math teacher how my grade is and see if there are extra credit options
- o   Ask coach if I qualified for the track meet

Friday

- o   Check planner and online classrooms for assignments
- o   Check grades for last week to make sure everything is done

Saturday

- o   Make time to talk to Yuki about that thing with Michael

Your Self-Monitoring Reminders

Sunday

o _____

o _____

Monday

o _____

o _____

Tuesday

o _____

o _____

Wednesday

○ _____

○ _____

Thursday

○ _____

○ _____

Friday

○ _____

○ _____

Saturday

○ _____

○ _____

Taking Time for Yourself

With all the work of everyday life, it's crucial to take time to care for yourself. Feeling rested and calm will help you get through your to-do list and allow you to focus more fully when you need to.

1. **Know your body's alarms.** Each person has an alarm system in their body that goes off when they begin to feel stressed. Recognizing this warning system is the body's way of alerting us that we're overwhelmed and need to take a minute to calm our nerves. These alarms may include tightness in the chest, fast breathing, or increased heart rate. Others feel hot and sweaty, particularly around the neck, ears, palms, and feet. Some people get headaches, stomach pain, and nausea. They may find their thoughts are racing, feel like avoiding work, or notice they're generally feeling "off." Start looking out for your alarms as a way to know when to take a little time for yourself.

2. **Find calming activities.** Find activities that help you feel relaxed and recharged. This is different for everyone, but popular strategies include meditating, watching a TV show or YouTube video, using adult coloring books, playing video games, reading, taking a shower or bath, going for a walk, playing with your pets, talking to a friend, shopping, exercising, cooking, or listening to a podcast. Remember to set a timer, since too much downtime can turn into avoidance, making it hard to get things done.

3. **Give yourself permission to relax.** It's better to take time to relax when we need it rather than to wait until we feel even more overwhelmed and nervous. Even if we plan for downtime and know it will help in the long run, we can feel guilty when there are still tasks to do. Try thinking of it this way: Taking time for yourself is like stopping at the gas station to fill up your tank. Sure, it feels inconvenient

sometimes, especially if you have somewhere to be. However, if you don't stop, you might end up running on fumes and eventually breaking down. See this relaxing time as filling up your emotional tank to rest up for your next trip.

Life Hack:
Just like the rest of your activities, downtime is important to plan for. If you schedule it into your day and add it to your to-do list, you're more likely to take part in relaxing, both because you'll be reminded to do it, and because it helps you acknowledge how important it is.

Key Takeaways:
Know your body's alarms and remember that they're alerting you to take a few minutes for yourself.

Plan times for relaxation into your day, and don't underestimate its importance. Just make sure you set a timer so you know when it's time to get back to work.

Know your go-to activities that help you relax and recharge.

Handling Hard Feelings (Including Being Kind to Yourself)

Everyone faces hard feelings, and we all have to figure out the best way to deal with them. Consider using a few of the following tips when your emotions become overwhelming.

1. **Take a break.** When you find yourself struggling with big emotions, it's okay to take a break. At home, go to a calm and quiet space. If you're in school, check to see if there is a counselor's office or a nurse you can visit, or duck into the bathroom for a minute. If you're with a friend, say you have to run outside to call home. This will give you a few moments to help your brain and your body calm down.

2. **Talk to yourself the way you would talk to a friend.** We are often much kinder to friends than we are to ourselves. Similarly, it's much easier to feel better if you're kind to yourself rather than hard on yourself for feeling down. For example, if you're upset because you got into a fight with a friend, instead of saying to yourself, "I can't believe I did that, he will never speak to me again!" try telling yourself, "I made a mistake, but I am only human," or, "I'll apologize. We've been friends for years, so hopefully he'll understand."

3. **Talk to someone.** If you need a little help, talk to a trusted friend, family member, teacher, or counselor. Often, those who are outside of the situation can help soothe our big emotions by validating us, comforting us, and offering advice if we need it.

4. **Think it through.** Thinking things through when we're upset is so challenging because of our brain's biological reaction to hard feelings: When the brain senses something that it perceives as danger, it automatically assesses the threat and prepares the body for fight, flight, or freeze. All

this happens before we have a chance to use logic. First, try breathing, taking breaks, and getting support from friends and family to calm the part of the brain that deals with big feelings. Then try to think about what's bothering you and potential solutions to the issue. If you want someone else's perspective, run your ideas by someone you trust to make sure you're on the right path.

Life Hack:
If you want to talk to someone but worry they're going to give advice you don't want, try saying, "I really need to talk, but I just want you to listen and be there. I think I can figure it out on my own, and right now I just need you to listen for a minute."

Key Takeaways:
Take some time to calm down and get your thinking brain back online. Once you do this, it will be easier to think things through.

Try being kind to yourself throughout the process.

If you're having a hard time, talk it out with someone you trust.

What Do You Think?
Have you ever had an overwhelming feeling and were hard on yourself about how you reacted? What kinds of thoughts could you use to be nicer to yourself? How could you handle it differently next time? Whom could you talk to next time you're feeling like that?

SOFIA'S DAY

Sofia is one week away from the start of her exams at the end of the quarter, and the pressure is on. Her parents tell her every day to study and lecture her about "wasted time" whenever she picks up her phone. She feels like she can't do anything right, everything is frustrating her, and even her tutor rambles on about "being more prepared." She also doesn't know where to start with the exam prep. Whenever she looks at her study guides, she gets totally overwhelmed and feels anxious and confused. The more this happens, the more down on herself she becomes. If everyone around you thinks you're lazy and you're not trying hard enough, eventually you start to believe them.

All this is making it hard to focus and study, and it's literally the last thing in the world Sofia wants to do. She'll find any excuse to get out of it, and when she does sit down to study, she just stares at the computer without doing any real work. Basically, she feels awful, stressed, and unprepared.

Sofia's best friend Jordan notices something is up and asks Sofia if she's okay. "Honestly, no," Sofia starts, and lays it all out for Jordan. "Wow," Jordan says, "that's a lot. My parents are on me about school, too. Have you told them you're feeling this way?"

Sofia thinks about it. She usually tries to keep everything in, which means she bottles it up until she freaks out at her parents, and they seem shocked that she feels this way. "I mean, not really," Sofia answers. "They just don't understand." Jordan agrees, saying, "It's hard to get through to my parents, too, but lately I have been trying to just say what I'm thinking. Instead of waiting and exploding, I figured I might as well try to deal with things as they come up. Honestly, it was my mom's idea. So now as soon as something bothers me, I actually talk to them about it, especially when I'm stressed out. Apparently, my parents just thought I had a bad attitude and didn't realize I was overwhelmed and needed some help. I swear they have turned into different humans since I started doing this."

Sofia was skeptical at first, but it was worth a shot. That night, she told her mom, "School sucks, and I feel like I can't do anything right. I don't even know where to start." Her mom, calm because Sofia wasn't yelling, replied, "I didn't know you felt that way. You do have a lot on your plate—how can I help?"

From there, Sofia was able to work stuff out with her mom's help. It may not work every time, but at least now her mom knows what's going on with her. And somehow, that made Sofia feel better.

Going with the Flow

"Going with the flow" simply means being flexible and changing plans when we need to. You're probably asked to be flexible often, whether it's going somewhere you don't want to, changing plans to accommodate a friend, or eating the dinner your mom made even if you aren't in the mood for it.

1. **Think flexibly.** Change is hard. Even the best changes take time to wrap our heads around (for example, getting into a dream college and learning to live away from home). When we loosen up our idea of what "should" or "has to" be, it's easier to deal with what *is*. If you find yourself using words like "should," "must," "have to," "always," or "never," you might be experiencing rigid thinking. Try to replace those words with "could," "might," "maybe," and "sometimes" to increase your flexibility. For example, see if you can shift the thought, "I have to do this science project with Miguel" to a more flexible plan, like, "I want to work with Miguel because he's my friend, but I guess I could work with Sam because he seems alright."

2. **Figure out what is most important.** Imagine you're talking with a friend about hanging out this weekend, and they invite two other people you didn't really want to see. Could you be flexible and hang out anyway, or would you rather cancel your plans? If it's more important to see your friend and you don't mind the extra company, be flexible and go with the flow. If you know the other kids are going to ruin your night, stick to what's important to you and hang out with your friend another time.

3. **Find tricks for transitions.** Transition means moving from one thing to another. This could be small—like going from relaxing to doing homework—or big, like moving from high school to college. We experience many transitions

every day, some we like (from homework to video games), and some not-so-great (from cozy bed to loud school bus). Flexible thinking helps a lot in those switches that are less enjoyable. Try thoughts like, "Ending my video games and getting started on homework is always easier than I think it will be" or, "It's cold out and I don't want to get out of bed, but I can wear my new sweats." Thinking about the next time you will be able to get back to what you want, like picking up the video game or climbing back in bed, also helps with transitions.

Life Hack:

If you're disappointed and find yourself being less than flexible, take a deep breath. Think about alternative solutions and try to compromise if you can.

Key Takeaways:

Use helpful thoughts to move from rigid to flexible thinking.

Take a minute to think of compromises to help you go with the flow.

Transitions are hard but can be made easier by thinking about the positive and planning the next time you can get back to what you want to do.

PART 3

Executive Skills Q&A

This section will answer common questions teens have about executive functioning skills and should help you put your strategies to work. I regularly hear these concerns in my practice and often work with teens to solve these and similar problems. The answers outlined here are quick and practical, and they give you a few tools you can implement right away. Some of the answers may look familiar, as you've already learned many of the strategies in part 2.

Q: I can never remember my assignments, and even when I do them, I forget to turn them in. Everyone says to use a planner, but I usually forget to use that, too. How can I get better at remembering this stuff?

A: It sounds like it could help to set a few reminders to lighten the load on your working memory.

1. Try setting alerts for your assignments. If your school allows you to use your phone, instead of writing your assignments in your planner, enter them directly into your calendar. Set an alarm when you're supposed to start your work, as well as an alert to turn your work in when class starts each day. Check your calendar before you get ready for bed each night and make sure to move any incomplete items to a future time when you can get back to them.

2. If you're having trouble figuring out exactly when to put something in your calendar, try a list app instead. (There are a few app suggestions in the resources section on page 115.) Enter items as soon as you think of them. That way you can check off what you have done and keep a running tab of your outstanding assignments.

Q: *I want to hang out with my friends, but I never think to make plans until the last minute. By then, they're usually busy. What can I do to plan ahead?*

A: **Remembering to make plans ahead of time is hard when you have so many other things to juggle, like school, homework, and extracurriculars.**

1. Set a routine. Pick a time to text your friends every week to ask them what their weekend plans are. If you know that you reach out to a friend every Thursday at 7 p.m., it will become a habit. That means you'll be less likely to forget.

2. If you see a friend at school who you want to make plans with, ask them right then and there. That way you avoid having to remember later on. You can also set a reminder in your calendar to text and follow up, or ask your friend to call you.

Q: I consider myself a friendly person, and I have no problem meeting people and making friends. For some reason, it's much harder to keep the same friends for a while. I feel like people don't call me back after we hang out a few times. My dad says that I need to be more interested in what the other kids like and talk less about myself, but I don't really know how.

A: It's common to get really excited about our own interests and want to share them with others. When we are so busy talking, we can often miss out on our friend's cues and don't realize when they aren't interested.

1. It's important to self-monitor and take a moment to notice the body language of friends. They may begin to look away, take deep breaths, move farther from you, or even roll their eyes if they're bored with the conversation. If you realize that you've been talking about your interests for a while or are taking too much charge of the conversation, perhaps try to shift the topic to something you know your friend likes.

2. *You* know that your friends are important to you, but it can be hard or even awkward to let them know how much you value them. Asking questions is one of the best ways to show others that you're interested and engaged. Try asking a question related to something you know about your friends, like a recent trip or favorite activity. Make sure you listen to their answers so that you can ask follow-up questions or make comments about what they're saying. It's tempting to simply add in our own experiences, but make sure you're listening to what your friends are saying rather than just waiting for your turn to talk.

Q: I want to get a new computer, but my mom says that I can't have it because I don't take care of my things. My room is a disaster zone but cleaning it up just feels like such a waste of time. Plus, it's mind-numbingly boring. What can I do?

A: Keeping a clean and organized room is hard, especially when you don't feel motivated or are busy with other things. Let's think about a few habits that might help.

1. Try making it a little more fun. Put on music or a good TV show (if you can pay attention to both). Maybe listen to a podcast while you work so taking care of your room doesn't feel so boring.

2. Do small chunks of cleaning at a time. For example, you could fold laundry on Sunday afternoons and organize your papers every Monday. Tasks feel easier with practice and less overwhelming if you do them bit by bit.

3. Set up a system that works for you. If you like where your belongings are and have a place for them all, tidying up will be quicker and you won't have to figure out where to put things.

Q: When my eight-year-old brother is around, he is so annoying. I go from chill to angry in five seconds. I don't love the way I act toward him, but I feel like he's baiting me, and I can't keep my cool. How can I stop getting angry so quickly?

A: Siblings can be annoying, especially when they know exactly how to push your buttons. It might be helpful to think of a few ways to calm down when you're feeling heated.

1. Ask for a family meeting. Sometimes you need a little extra help from parental authorities to work things out. In this meeting, let everyone speak about their idea of the problem first, then offer potential solutions one by one. Make sure that no one is interrupted, even when there are disagreements. This will allow everyone to feel heard and will help you reach a positive outcome. Try to compromise on a solution or two everyone can agree on, and then test it out for a week. Finally, come back together next week to work out the kinks.

2. Know that your brother is pushing your buttons for a reason. Maybe he'd like to play with you, or maybe he wants to make sure he has your attention. Could you talk to him and see if there's a time you can hang out without him getting under your skin?

3. If your brother isn't willing to talk things out, how could you get yourself out of the situation? Go to a place where he can't follow you, like your room, to cool down and take a deep breath. If he keeps following you, can you find a room with a locked door, like a bathroom, just to get away for a minute?

Q: *My family always talks about how sensitive I am. I feel like I'm just reacting to what they're doing, but maybe I am more emotional than I should be. I want to have a thicker skin, but it feels impossible. What can I do to toughen up a little?*

A: *This is a hard question, and unfortunately, I hear it a lot. Being emotional and having strong feelings doesn't mean that you are too sensitive; it means that you feel things deeply. There's nothing wrong with this, and in fact, you may have already noticed that the more you fight your feelings or try to get rid of them, the stronger they become. That's because the way to really soothe ourselves is to acknowledge and validate our emotions instead of beating ourselves up for having them. No one ever felt better by hearing, "Just calm down," but it does help to hear, "That is the worst; I would feel that way, too."*

Still, in the moment you may wish you had more control over your reaction to these feelings. If this is the case, think about healthy ways to express yourself. Could you talk to a trusted friend, write in a journal, or spend some time by yourself? It might help to find something distracting for a while, like petting your dog or watching TV. This time and space may be what you need to let yourself feel down or angry while still responding in a way that you'd like to.

Q: *My teacher pulled me aside yesterday and told me that she thinks I'm too distractible, and she's worried that I am not paying attention. I try, but sometimes I daydream, especially during long lectures. What should I do when I just can't seem to focus?*

A: **Many students daydream during class. If you're finding that it's getting in the way of your ability to learn, try a few of these tips:**

1. Write down what your teacher is saying, as they're saying it. Taking notes keeps your head in the game because it forces you to listen in order to write.

2. If you have a watch with a vibrate setting, set the timer for five-minute intervals throughout the classes that you have the hardest time concentrating in. These can serve as reminders to check back into class if you need to.

3. Put away your distractions. If you have a laptop or device you're using in class to take notes, try paper and pencil instead. It's too easy to get distracted on our devices, which makes it twice as hard to pay attention and avoid daydreaming.

Q: I want to do well in school and do what my parents ask, but I really have a hard time getting started on tasks that I'm not interested in. How can I motivate myself to get started?

A: Task initiation (i.e., getting started) can be hard when we're not so interested in the task at hand. There are a few things you can do to make this easier on yourself:

1. Think of rewards for after you're done. These may be natural rewards—like your room is clean and therefore you can find that pair of jeans you've been looking for. Or they can be rewards you set for yourself—like you're going to make those brownies you've been thinking about all day as soon as your history packet is done. Either way, setting rewards for the end of the activity can be just the motivation you need to get started.

2. Break your work down into smaller chunks. This can be set amounts of time, like 15- to 20-minute intervals of work, or by task, like three math problems and then a break. Smaller tasks feel less overwhelming and are often easier to start.

Q: My dad asks me every day to do my chores, and I say okay, but then I don't. We get into big fights, and I wish I could find a way that we could all be happy. How can I handle this?

A: A lot of teens want to make their parents happy, but the desire to relax instead of doing chores is a hard one to ignore.

1. Spend some time talking to your parents about this issue. Explain the fact that you do want them to be happy and that you understand why you need to do chores, but that it's hard to get yourself going on them. Brainstorm together about a compromise or reward system that may make everyone happier.

2. Make a list with your parents of all the chores they'd like done in the house. Then pick three or four to do each week. For example, you could choose taking out the trash every Thursday night, washing the dishes after dinner, and tidying up the family room on Sunday afternoons before your video game match with friends. Incorporate these into your calendar. Picking the chores you want instead of having them assigned to you gives you more control over the situation, which makes you more likely to follow through.

Q: *I have lost my keys three times already this year. My mom says if I keep losing them, she's going to take away privileges, since the replacements are getting expensive. How can I stop losing important things?*

A: **It's frustrating to not know where your things are, and I'm sure you don't want your mom to take away your privileges. Try using a few tricks to keep track of your things.**

1. Be mindful of where you tend to keep your keys. If they're in your pocket or the open zipper pouch of a backpack, they're more likely to fall out without you noticing. Instead, zip them into your backpack or clip them in a secure location to avoid losing them.

2. If you're in your house, ask for a basket by the front door. Make a habit of tossing your keys in the same place every time you come inside. Practice this for a few weeks and you'll likely notice that it becomes automatic to throw them in the basket, thus cutting down the chance of losing them.

3. For keeping track outside the house, try a locator device that beeps, like a Tile. This will allow you to use your phone to locate your keys through a device that is on the key ring.

Q: *There are days when I have so many assignments from different classes that I don't know where to start. What are some ways I can learn to prioritize my work when it all feels a little overwhelming?*

A: **Picking a starting point is about weighing the importance of one activity against another. Ask yourself a few of the questions below to make decisions about prioritizing easier and quicker.**

1. Start by asking yourself, "What's due first?" If you have two assignments, start with the one that's due sooner. Most people know that anything due the next day goes straight to the top of the list. But what about when nothing is due right away? Begin with the work that's due soonest, and schedule in time to focus on other assignments later. Make sure you don't wait until the last second.

2. If you have limited time or two assignments are due on the same day, ask yourself the following questions to help you prioritize: How much of my grade does this count for? In which class do I have a lower grade, and can I bring it up by focusing my energy there? How can I direct my efforts to make the most impact on my grades? Can I ask my family or a friend to help me figure out which is the most important? Answering these questions may help clarify where you need to focus your energy.

Q: *I really want to do well in my classes, but sometimes people think I'm lazy or unmotivated just because I have trouble with executive functioning. How can I explain to people that I care and my struggles are not related to being lazy?*

A: **First of all, I'm glad that you realize that you are not lazy or unmotivated. Remember, not saying anything is always an option if you're not comfortable. If you do want to talk to people about executive functioning skills, clarify that they have nothing to do with intelligence or your desire to achieve. Give examples of EF skills, like planning, organizing, and task initiation, and explain that each of us has varying strengths and needs. You can also talk about how the prefrontal cortex (i.e., the EF part of the brain) keeps growing until our mid-20s.**

If you know the person well, you may also be able to ask them what EF skills they find easy and difficult in their lives. Of course, the closer the relationship, the more open and honest you can be about your own ways of developing these skills. If you don't know the person well, or know that they may not be the best person to talk to, you can simply say, "I am working on it," or say nothing at all.

Q: *The other day I went to the store to look for a certain pair of jeans. They were out of my size, so my dad suggested that I look into another style. I got really upset and felt like no other jeans would do, and we ended up having to leave because I was too angry to try on anything else. Is there a way I could be more flexible once I have my mind set on something?*

A: **Once we set our mind on something, especially something we're excited about, it can be really hard to change plans because we feel so disappointed. Flexible thinking and emotion regulation skills may help in this case.**

1. First, do something to calm your body and mind down a bit. It's much harder to use logic and reasoning when you're upset. Start with a few deep breaths in through your nose and out through your mouth, making sure you expand your belly with each inhalation. You can also try other ways to help soothe your body through calming and distraction, such as taking a walk or texting a friend.

2. Once you feel your heart rate reducing and you're a bit calmer, think about why you are most disappointed. In this situation, maybe you were really looking forward to wearing those jeans to a party this weekend, or you've been saving for them for a long time. Talk to your dad about this, and see if there's another solution, like ordering them online or going to another store. Once you're calm, it's much easier to think flexibly about your problems.

Q: *The other day my best friend and I got into a big fight because she wanted to go to the movies, and I told her we needed to go a party with all our friends. I know I need to be flexible, but am I wrong in telling her what I want to do?*

A: **You are never wrong to speak your mind and stand up for yourself, as long as you're still respecting the rights of others. Having a voice is critical, but just as important is allowing your friend space to discuss her opinions as well.**

1. When having a disagreement, try to calm yourself down first before getting too deep into the woods. When you're angry or upset, you may feel sad, defensive, or shut down. None of that helps a conversation, so it's best to take a breath or a break if you need to.

2. Once you feel a little calmer, ask the person questions about where they're coming from. Curiosity often makes anger and annoyance dissipate, and it's easier to come to a compromise if you understand your friend's point of view.

3. After you ask your friend questions, listen to and acknowledge what they say. In arguments, we're tempted to get our point across and make people see our perspective, but this doesn't always move the conversation to a point of resolution. After you respond, see if you can help your friend see your side, in a calm way. It may sound something like, "I hear that you really wanted to go to the movies, and I get that you were looking forward to it. I really want to see that one, too. But I also really wanted to go to that party because I wanted to be with everyone all together. Could we go to the movies tomorrow? I'll buy popcorn!"

Q: My parents are always reminding me to do things, like homework, chores, and calling friends to make plans. I prefer to do them on my own, and I wish they would just trust me. How do I let them know that I can handle things?

A: Parents worry, which is not a news flash, I'm sure. However, they're more likely to loosen the reins if they feel like they can trust you to get stuff done.

1. Most likely, your parents *want* you to be more independent. They don't want to keep track of your stuff in addition to their own to-do list. However, they probably keep tabs on you because they worry that you'll forget things and want to protect you from the consequences of not getting your stuff done. Ask them to talk with you about this, and brainstorm ways you can have more freedom together.

2. They may be more likely to give you independence if you show them that you have a plan. Let them know how you'll keep track of your work and set reminders for yourself, and maybe even offer to check in with them for weekly updates. That way they can ease up and you can get more freedom. The longer it goes well, the more freedom you will likely get.

Q: Sometimes I feel down about my executive functioning skills. It seems like things that are easy for everyone else are just so much harder for me. I was thinking it might be good to talk to a therapist or counselor about it, but how do I even get started?

A: You're right; feeling like you have to work so much harder than your peers can be discouraging. The fact that you're thinking about talking to someone, like a counselor or therapist, shows that you care about your mental health and know that working through challenges with someone is a lot easier than trying to handle them all on your own. If you think your parents would be receptive, start there. Tell them you're having a tough time and ask if they can help you find a local therapist or counselor to talk to. If you're worried they might not be able to help, call one of the helplines you'll find in "How to Ask For Help" (see page 18) and in the resources section (see page 115). Or, try talking to the counselor at your school. They're free, available, and trained to help students get through tough times.

Q: I have a big exam coming up, and I want to study efficiently. Do you have any good study tips?

A: Big exams mean big stress. It's great that you're thinking about starting early. You can find an outline for study tools and an organizer to help plan out your time on pages 50 and 51, respectively. Additionally, let's think about a few techniques that might help.

1. Start early and don't wait until the week before to look at the study guide. Plan out several weeks to review at your own pace without feeling anxious or rushed.

2. Follow the study guide from your teacher or make your own study guide based on the material you've learned that semester. This will keep you on track and ensure you're aware of the information you should focus on.

3. Check in with the teacher as you start to study. Let them know your current plan and ask them if they think there's anything you should add. Most times, teachers are happy to help and discuss this with you.

Q: *I want to be able to participate in class discussions, but I find myself getting distracted or anxious, both of which make it hard to give good input. What should I do to make sure I can focus on what everyone else is saying, and how can I calm myself down when I get nervous?*

A: **Most people get nervous talking in front of big groups, especially when they're people you know and have to see every day. Start with techniques to calm your body down, and then focus on attending to what your classmates are saying.**

1. Take a deep breath and slow your heart rate as much as you can. Know that it's normal to feel a little amped when you have to talk in front of your class. Be kind to yourself and remember that all you can do is try.

2. Just like you, people are usually paying more attention to themselves and their own worries than they are to you. Most people focus on themselves and their own nerves during class discussions, which should take some of the pressure off you!

3. Shift your focus to what your classmates are saying by taking notes. This will force your brain to concentrate on the discussion and will also get your head into the classroom rather than thinking about your nerves.

Q: Applying to college is stressful! I need a better system to keep track of all the parts of the application and to manage the whole process. What should I do?

A: Applications are stressful because the outcomes are so important to us. It's great that you want to figure out a way to make sure you have everything you need organized and ready to go.

1. Make folders, either on the computer or physically. Label a folder for each school you're applying to and put a list of everything you need for that school in each one. For example, you may need a transcript, three letters of recommendation, a personal statement, three supplemental essays, and your demographic information for one school. Make a checklist and check off each item as you send it in to the school.

2. Create a calendar for deadlines. Write when each application is due and when you will hear back (for motivation). Add times to work on the applications in the calendar as well, so you won't feel rushed near the end.

3. Make sure to ask for recommendations well in advance, to give your references time to complete them and send them in before the deadline.

Q: I never used to make my own appointments, but now that I'm 18, my mom wants me to arrange them on my own. I have to figure out how to get a doctor's appointment because I need some paperwork signed before I go to school in the fall. Where do I start?

A: To make a doctor's appointment, it will help you to know what to say. Think about these steps:

1. Practice what you'll say with a parent. A good start is "Hello, my name is _____. I would like to make an appointment with Dr. _____ for a regular checkup. I need this before I go to college in September." When you call the office, they'll likely ask you for your date of birth to find your file and set up your appointment. You can also request specific days and times that work better for you, but it's best to have your calendar handy in case other times are offered.

2. Ask the receptionist if you need to bring anything to the appointment, as well as the address and time you should be there. If the visit is virtual, make sure you have the link and the time you are supposed to log on. Write this down and make a calendar appointment with reminders the week before, the day before, and an hour before to avoid forgetting.

Q: I really like video games and watching videos on my phone, but I'll admit that I get sucked in for hours. How do I stop myself and get off the games so I can feel more productive?

A: Games are designed to make it hard to stop, and videos are often on auto-play, making it easy to watch "just one more" over and over again.

1. Set a timer or an automatic shutoff. There are apps that help shut down our screen time and remind us to take breaks. Making the break automatic will help you turn off the screens.

2. If you want to know how much time you're spending and track your progress, download a screen time app that can track your overall phone time, as well as hours logged in every app.

3. If you are playing games to avoid doing something (especially if you are stressed about the task), think about other ways to manage your worries. Start by acknowledging that you might be avoiding a hard task, then break it down into manageable chunks, and reward yourself when you are done.

Q: I know that breaks and rewards are good motivators, but I can't come up with them in the moment. Can you make a few suggestions?

A: First, think about what you like, as this will be the best way to find motivators. Here are a few categories to pick from:

1. Activities: Watching TV, playing sports or games, doing a puzzle, taking the dogs for a walk, making something creative, reading, cooking, enjoying screen time, and more. Allot time for activities you like as a reward.

2. Time with others: Sometimes you may have to do solo activities that aren't your favorite, like homework or piano practice. Plan for time with friends or family afterward to motivate yourself.

3. Items: You can pick your own items or make a deal with your parents for rewards. This may be something small, like a favorite dessert, or a larger reward, like a video game or a gift card to your favorite store.

Q: Sometimes people tell me that I act without thinking. Can you tell me more about how to slow down and strengthen my impulse control?

A: Impulse control means taking a minute to stop and think before you act. Try a few strategies to practice this EF skill.

1. Before you make a decision, count to 10. This will give your brain a moment to kick on your prefrontal cortex and think about your actions.

2. Try the "better or worse" trick. If you find yourself acting impulsively, ask yourself, "Will this make things better or worse?" If the answer is worse, take a minute and consider other choices.

3. Think about what you would say to a friend who is planning on doing what you're about to do. Might you advise them against it, or tell them to think about how their actions may impact them in the future? If so, try to apply that advice to yourself.

Q: My parents expect me to be on top of everything, like knowing my grades, remembering when track practice is, and checking in with my piano teacher about my progress. I say I will, but when the time comes, it doesn't even occur to me to ask. I usually find out after it's too late and then I get in trouble. Why is it so hard for me to think about how I'm doing in the moment?

A: Self-monitoring—checking in on ourselves and seeing how things are going—can be easy to forget, especially as life gets busy. Sometimes things that aren't mandatory get lost in the shuffle, especially as we're developing our working memory.

1. Go easy on yourself when you do forget. Being hard on yourself usually won't motivate behavior change. Instead, acknowledge that you're disappointed and think about a plan for next time.

2. Think about checking in on your progress as a required assignment. By making it "mandatory" for yourself, you're more likely to remember. Then incorporate it into a routine, add it to your to-do list, or put it in your calendar.

3. Set an alert on your phone to send an email to your teacher or to check in with them after class. That way it will be harder to forget.

Q: My friends get really annoyed with me because I'm always late. Last week we missed the first 10 minutes of a movie because I was late, and I could tell they were angry. What can I do to be on time?

A: Being late every once in a while is to be expected. It sounds like your friends are frustrated because you're consistently late. Sometimes when we're chronically late, our friends feel like we don't value their time, or they get annoyed when they miss important events. Most of us do not mean to send that signal, and there are a few things we can do to help this habit.

1. Apologize to your friends. If you're close with them, consider letting them know that you're working on it and that you value their patience.

2. Set multiple alerts on your phone. The trick is not waiting until you need to leave to set the alarm. Start with an alert two hours before you have to go, then one hour, and even 30 minutes before you need to leave. That way you won't be surprised when it's time to get out the door.

3. Think about how long it realistically takes you to get ready. Many people get distracted, but they also underestimate the time it takes to get going. Account for all the tasks you need to do, like showering, brushing your teeth, picking an outfit, doing your hair, and getting gas. The little things are often the ones that cause us to run 10 to 15 minutes behind.

On the Road to Success

I hope that after reading this book, learning the EF techniques, and thinking about how you can integrate them into your life, you feel more confident and prepared. Just knowing about the executive functions—along with the tools you can use to build them—puts you on the road to success. You have at your fingertips strategies to help you achieve your goals. The more you practice, the more success you'll experience, and the greater your confidence will be.

With a little preparation, areas of growth can turn into strengths. Remember, we do not expect mastery after using a strategy once or twice. We gain skills through small, consistent efforts over time. Think of something you find easy, almost automatic. You may think it's no big deal now, but do you remember how you felt when you first started? There was probably excitement, fear, trepidation, and frustration. Just like learning to play the drums or ride a bike, developing your EF skills takes many practice sessions which usually prove to be simultaneously frustrating and rewarding.

One of my favorite sayings is: "You can't walk 30 minutes into the woods and get out in five." Basically, it means that you can't expect to change overnight. Use the tools in this book as a compass when you move through the woods and feel like you don't know which way to turn. They're meant to support, guide, and point you in the right direction.

Implement the parts that work for you and modify strategies as necessary. There's no need for memorization, as you can flip to the relevant section of the book anytime. Return to the pages whenever you need a little help. You may even notice a new trick that you didn't see before.

Finally, remember the amazing strengths you already possess. Whether you're creative, intuitive, inventive, energetic, or empathic, harness those strengths as you work toward your executive functioning goals.

Resources for Teens

Here are a few resources you can use to learn more and build skills in executive functioning. You can also look in the app store on your phone to find even more tools. Test a few out to find ones that work for you.

Google Calendar

This app syncs with your Google email and makes it easy to quickly add appointments and track your days. Keep your calendars color coded for each of your events: school, sports, chores, etc.

Evernote

This app allows you to make lists and calendar reminders in a variety of templates, including daily, monthly, and yearly calendars, to-do lists, journal prompts, meeting notes, and more. You can also save articles and information from online sources directly into the app, as well as set timers and share with others.

Productive

This app allows you to add new goals, for both weekly and one-time tasks. It can be motivating as it tracks your progress. It encourages planning by helping you set days and times for each habit and create reminder alerts.

Homework

The Homework app allows you to make a folder for each class, track when assignments are due, enter a number of details like the type of task (presentation, test, etc.), attach related images, and set reminders.

The Child Mind Institute

This organization provides scientific information about executive functioning in articles that are succinct and accessible. Find info at childmind.org/topics/concerns/executive-function.

If you need help:

Call the Teen Line from 6:00 p.m. to 10:00 p.m. Pacific Time at 310-855-4673 or text "TEEN" to 839863.

Call the National Suicide Prevention Lifeline anytime at 1-800-273-8255.

Resources for Parents

Below are resources for parents to gain additional information on executive functioning as well as parent support.

Center on the Developing Child, Harvard University

Harvard has vast research on executive functioning and has developed an activities guide entitled "Enhancing and Practicing Executive Function Skills with Children from Infancy to Adolescence." developingchild.harvard.edu/resources/activities-guide-enhancing-and-practicing-executive-function-skills-with-children-from-infancy-to-adolescence.

Understood.org

This website has information, ideas, and printable resources to assist in building EF skills. Use the search bar to find specific topics of interest for your teen.

The Child Mind Institute

This is listed in the resources for teens section, and is helpful for parents as well. You can explore this site with your child or use the information as a jumping-off point to engage in a conversation about EF skills. childmind.org/topics/concerns/executive-function.

Smart but Scattered Teens: The "Executive Skills" Program for Helping Teens Reach Their Potential by Richard Guare, PhD, Peg Dawson, EdD, and Colin Guare

This book serves as a guide for parents by providing ways to support smart teens who struggle with executive functioning skills.

References

Aben, Bart, Sven Stapert, and Arjan Blokland. "About the Distinction between Working Memory and Short-Term Memory." *Frontiers in Psychology* 3 (2012): 301.

ADHD Editorial Board. "What I Would Never Trade Away." Accessed March 28, 2020. additudemag.com/slideshows/positives-of-adhd.

American Academy of Child and Adolescent Psychiatry. "Teen Brain: Behavior, Problem Solving, and Decision Making." September 2016. aacap.org/AACAP/Families_and_Youth/Facts_for_Families/FFF-Guide /The-Teen-Brain-Behavior-Problem-Solving-and-Decision-Making-095.aspx.

Arnsten, Amy F. T. "Stress Signalling Pathways That Impair Prefrontal Cortex Structure and Function." *Nature Reviews Neuroscience* 10, no. 6 (2009): 410–422.

Barkley, Russell A. *Executive Functions: What They Are, How They Work, and Why They Evolved.* New York: Guilford Press, 2012.

Barlow, Ellen. "Under the Hood of the Adolescent Brain." Harvard Medical School News & Research. Last modified October 17, 2014. hms.harvard.edu /news/under-hood-adolescent-brain.

Blair, Clancy. "Developmental Science and Executive Function." *Current Directions in Psychological Science* 25, no. 1 (2016): 3–7.

Blum, Kenneth, Amanda Lih-Chuan Chen, Eric R. Braverman, David E. Comings, Thomas J. H. Chen, Vanessa Arcuri, Seth H. Blum, et al. "Attention-Deficit-Hyperactivity Disorder and Reward Deficiency Syndrome." *Neuropsychiatric Disease and Treatment* 4, no. 5 (2008): 893–917.

Brown, Thomas E. *Attention Deficit Disorder: The Unfocused Mind in Children and Adults.* New Haven: Yale University Press, 2005.

Center on the Developing Child: Harvard University. "What Is Executive Function? And How Does It Relate to Child Development.?" Accessed

February 23, 2020. developingchild.harvard.edu/resources/what-is
-executive-function-and-how-does-it-relate-to-child-development.

Center on the Developing Child: Harvard University. "Executive Function &
Self-Regulation." Accessed February 23, 2020. developingchild.harvard.edu
/science/key-concepts/executive-function.

Children and Adults with Attention-Deficit/Hyperactivity Disorder
(CHADD). "Executive Function Skills." Accessed February 23, 2020. chadd
.org/about-adhd/executive-function-skills.

Cowan, Nelson. "What Are the Differences between Long-Term, Short-Term,
and Working Memory?" *Progress in Brain Research* 169 (2008): 323–338.

Cuncic, Arlin. "Amygdala Hijack and the Fight or Flight Response." Med-
ically reviewed by Steven Gans, MD. *Verywell Mind.* October 16, 2019.
verywellmind.com/what-happens-during-an-amygdala-hijack-4165944.

Csikszentmihalyi, Mihaly. *Flow: The Psychology of Optimal Experience.*
New York: Harper & Row, 1990.

Dovis, Sebastiaan, Saskia Van der Oord, Reinout W. Wiers, and Pier J. M.
Prins. "Improving Executive Functioning in Children with ADHD: Training
Multiple Executive Functions within the Context of a Computer Game. A Ran-
domized Double-Blind Placebo Controlled Trial." *PloS One* 10, no. 4 (2015).

Eslinger, Paul J. "Conceptualizing, Describing, and Measuring Components
of Executive Function: A Summary." In *Attention, Memory, and Executive
Function,* edited by G. Reid Lyon & Norman A. Krasnegor, 367–395. Brookes
Publishing, 1996.

Faber, Adele, and Elaine Mazlish. *Siblings Without Rivalry: How to Help Your
Children Live Together So You Can Live Too.* New York: W. W. Norton, 2012.

Faber Taylor, Andrea, and Frances E. Kuo. "Children With Attention Deficits
Concentrate Better After Walk in the Park." *Journal of Attention Disorders*
12, no. 5 (2009): 402–409. doi.org/10.1177/1087054708323000.

Flippin, Royce. "Hyperfocus: The ADHD Phenomenon of Intense Fixation." *ADDitude: Inside the ADHD Mind.* March 2, 2020. additudemag.com /understanding-adhd-hyperfocus.

Fruzzetti, Alan E., Wendy Crook, Karen M. Erikson, Jung Eun Lee, and John M. Worrall. "Emotion Regulation." In *General Principles and Empirically Supported Techniques of Cognitive Behavior Therapy,* edited by William O'Donohue and Jane E. Fisher, 272–284. New York: Wiley, 2009.

Gioia, Gerard A., Peter K. Isquith, Steven C. Guy, and Lauren Kenworthy. *Behavior Rating Inventory of Executive Function: BRIEF.* Odessa, FL: Psychological Assessment Resources, 2000.

Hosenbocus, Sheik, and Raj Chahal. "A Review of Executive Function Deficits and Pharmacological Management in Children and Adolescents." *Journal of the Canadian Academy of Child and Adolescent Psychiatry* 21, no. 3 (2012): 223–229.

Hupfeld, Kathleen E., Tessa R. Abagis, and Priti Shah. "Living 'In the Zone': Hyperfocus in Adult ADHD." *ADHD Attention Deficit and Hyperactivity Disorders* 11, no. 2 (2019): 191–208.

Johns Hopkins Medicine. "Teenagers and Sleep: How Much Sleep Is Enough?" Accessed February 23, 2020. hopkinsmedicine.org/health /wellness-and-prevention/teenagers-and-sleep-how-much-sleep-is-enough.

Kimball, Harry. "Hyperfocus: The Flip Side of ADHD?" *Child Mind Institute.* Accessed February 28, 2020. childmind.org/article/hyperfocus-the-flip-side -of-adhd.

Kornell, Nate. "Optimising Learning Using Flashcards: Spacing Is More Effective Than Cramming." *Applied Cognitive Psychology: The Official Journal of the Society for Applied Research in Memory and Cognition* 23, no. 9 (2009): 1297–1317.

Levin, Ben. "20 Minutes to Change a Life?" *Phi Delta Kappan* 90, no. 5 (2009): 384.

Murray, Desiree W., and Katie Rosanbalm. "Promoting Self-Regulation in Adolescents and Young Adults: A Practice Brief. (OPRE Report 2015-82)." Washington, D.C.: Office of Planning, Research and Evaluation, Administration for Children and Families, U.S. Department of Health and Human Services (2017).

Nash, Kelly, Sara Stevens, Rachel Greenbaum, Judith Weiner, Gideon Koren, and Joanne Rovet. "Improving Executive Functioning in Children with Fetal Alcohol Spectrum Disorders." *Child Neuropsychology* 21, no. 2 (2015): 191–209.

National Scientific Council on the Developing Child National Forum on Early Childhood Policies and Programs. "Building the Brain's 'Air Traffic Control' Systems: How Early Experiences Shape the Development of Executive Functioning." Accessed March 6, 2020. developingchild.harvard .edu/wp-content/uploads/2011/05/How-Early-Experiences-Shape-the -Development-of-Executive-Function.pdf.

Needleman, Sarah E. "Videogame Developers Are Making It Harder to Stop Playing: Players Are Logging More Hours as Developers Find New Ways to Keep Them Engaged." *Wall Street Journal*. August 20, 2018. wsj.com /articles/wheres-the-off-switch-videogame-developers-are-making-it-harder -to-stop-playing-1534757400.

Parker, David R., Sharon Field Hoffman, Shlomo Sawilowsky, and Laura Rolands. "An Examination of the Effects of ADHD Coaching on University Students' Executive Functioning." *Journal of Postsecondary Education and Disability* 24, no. 2 (2011): 115–132.

Phillips, Lorian. "ADHD and Hyperfocus." *Mental Health Matters* 5, no. 6 (2018): 13–14.

Ryback, Ralph. "The Powerful Psychology Behind Cleanliness: How to Stay Organized and Reap the Health Benefits. July 11, 2016. psychologytoday.com /us/blog/the-truisms-wellness/201607/the-powerful-psychology -behind-cleanliness.

Steenari, Maija-Riikka, Virve Vuontela, E. Juulia Paavonen, Synnöve Carlson, Mika Fjällberg, and Eeva T. Aronen. "Working Memory and Sleep in 6- to 13-Year-Old Schoolchildren." *Journal of the American Academy of Child & Adolescent Psychiatry* 42, no. 1 (2003): 85–92.

Smith, Bryan. *What Were You Thinking? A Story About Learning To Control Your Impulses*. Nebraska: Boys Town Press, 2016.

Suchy, Yana. "Executive Functioning: Overview, Assessment, and Research Issues for Non-Neuropsychologists." *Annals of Behavioral Medicine* 37, no. 2 (2009): 106–116.

The Understood Team. "Why Kids With Executive Functioning Issues Have Trouble Starting Tasks." Accessed March 1, 2020. understood.org/en /learning-thinking-differences/child-learning-disabilities/executive -functioning-issues/why-kids-with-executive-functioning-issues-have -trouble-starting-tasks.

UCLA Health. "Sleep and Teens." Accessed March 9, 2020. uclahealth.org /sleepcenter/sleep-and-teens.

Index

A

Appointment making, 43, 58–59, 107, 115

B

Body language, 41, 70, 71, 90

Brain

adolescent brain development, 12

air traffic control system, 3–4

EF challenges, role in, 7

hard feelings, biological
reaction to, 80–81

note-taking and concentration, 105

prefrontal cortex, 2, 99, 110

working memory and, 10, 49

Breaks. *See* Timers, setting

C

Checklist, morning routine, 26–27

Chores

apps and, 32

EF tricks for completing, 66–67

getting done, 62–63

parents and, 96

room cleaning, 60–61

sample chore table, 64

sample to-do list, 35

Your Chore Table template, 65

College applications, 106

E

Emotion regulation

class discussions and, 40

defining, 3

flexible thinking and, 100

hard feelings, 80–81

homework and, 38–39

self-assessment, 13

strong emotions, dealing with, 12

thick skin, 93

Exams, studying for, 48–49, 50–51, 104

Executive functioning (EF)

defining, 2, 3–4

distractions and, 2, 4, 19, 38, 94

goals and, 4, 7, 115

help, resources for, 18, 103, 116

laziness accusations, 6, 82, 99

misperceptions, 6–7

prioritizing, 3, 4–6, 25, 33, 38, 39, 66–67, 98

talking and listening skills, 70–71, 90

transitions and, 3, 8, 84–85

F

Feelings. *See* Emotion regulation

Flexible thinking

adjustments and, 14

as an EF skill, 3, 66

calm body and mind, 100

class discussions, 40

friends, planning with, 68–69, 89, 101

going with the flow, 84–85

re-prioritizing, 33

rigid thinking, 85

self-assessment, 9

Focus

breaks and, 39, 52

calm and rested state, 78

class discussions, and, 40–41, 105

daydreaming and, 94

difficulties with, 82

EF skills, enhancing, 21

during group projects, 43

guidance on studying, 44, 45

hyperfocus, 6, 19

prioritizing and, 98

self-assessment, 19–20

study guides, usage, 104

timers and, focus, 53, 66

to-do lists, 33

Acknowledgments

I could not have written this book without the encouragement of my husband, Tim. Thank you for knowing that I could do it and reminding me of that when I forgot. Thank you to my family for being the best cheerleaders and my friends for sharing in my joy. Finally, thank you to my colleagues for your unyielding support and guidance.

About the Author

Laurie Chaikind McNulty, LCSW-C, is a clinical social worker with over a decade of experience working with children, adolescents, and families. She has worked in a number of settings supporting clients, including schools, outpatient hospital centers, and private practice. Laurie specializes in supporting people with developmental differences, with training as a Leadership Education in Neurodevelopmental and Related Disabilities (LEND) scholar. She applies her experience in education, research, graduate-level training, and clinical practice to supporting teens and young adults in enhancing their executive functioning. Laurie currently works at a private practice in Kensington, Maryland, and is a consultant for the National Institutes of Health. She lives in Brookeville, Maryland, with her husband and two dogs.

Printed in the USA
CPSIA information can be obtained
at www.ICGtesting.com
CBHW081058120224
R14898600001B/R148986PG4145CBX00010B/7

9 781647 396510